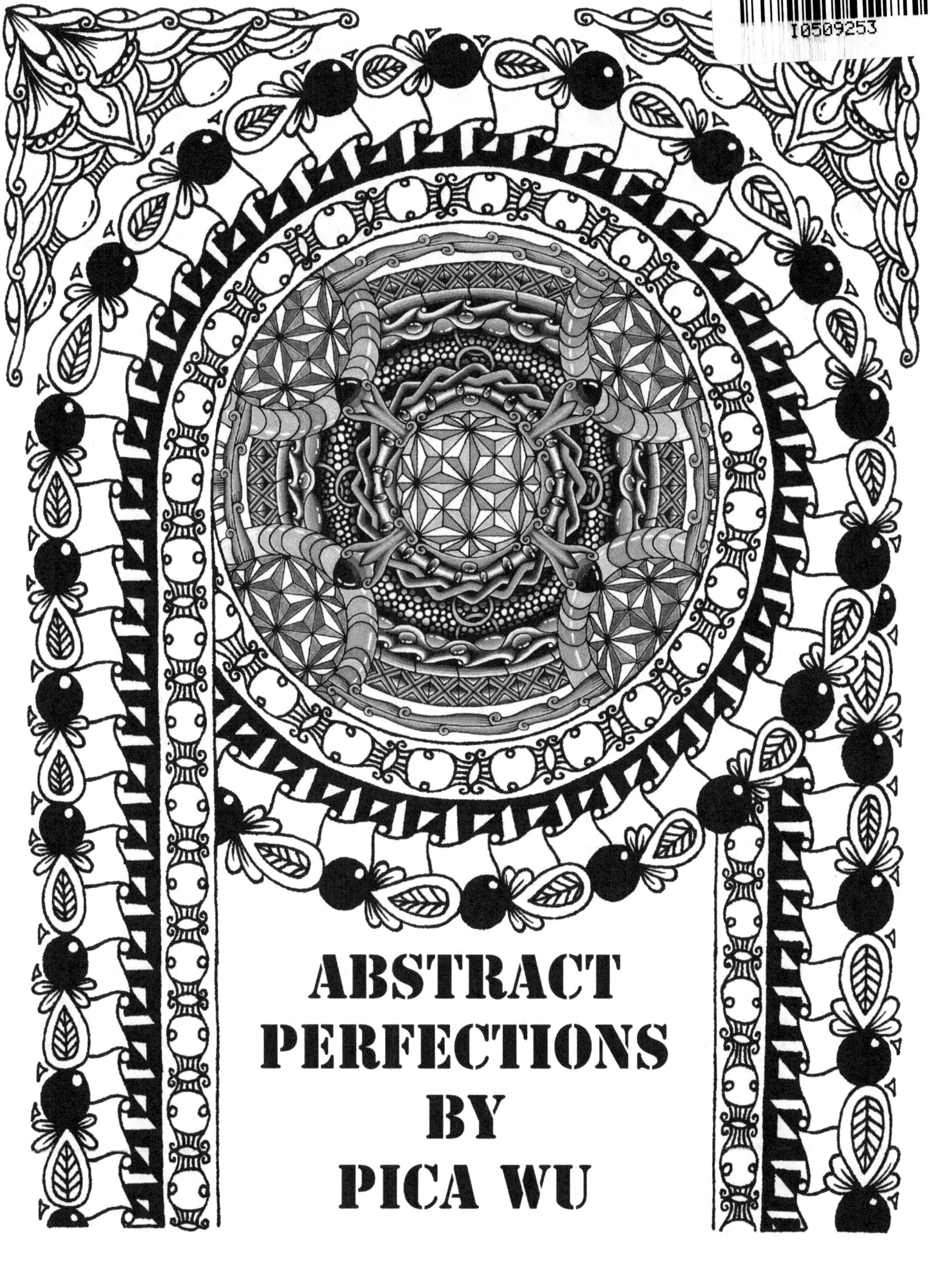

# ABSTRACT PERFECTIONS

BY

PICA WU

Published by "GDG©" Global Doodle Gems

*Share your colored versions with us ! We love seeing your results and hearing from you*
*we are social !*

The Official FB book page, stay on top of what we have in the works !
www.facebook.com/globaldoodlegems
The Community group, share your colored pages, meet the artists, enjoy exclusive freebies, take part in community Charity books and so much more......
www.facebook.com/groups/globaldoodlegems/
Follow us on Twitter.... @GlobalDoodlegem
We are on Instagram too
@globaldoodlegems for instagram
...and if you are not social like that we have a blog
globaldoodlegems.wordpress.com


All of us from the Global Doodle Gems wish you a colortastic time and look forward to seeing your wonderful color results online !

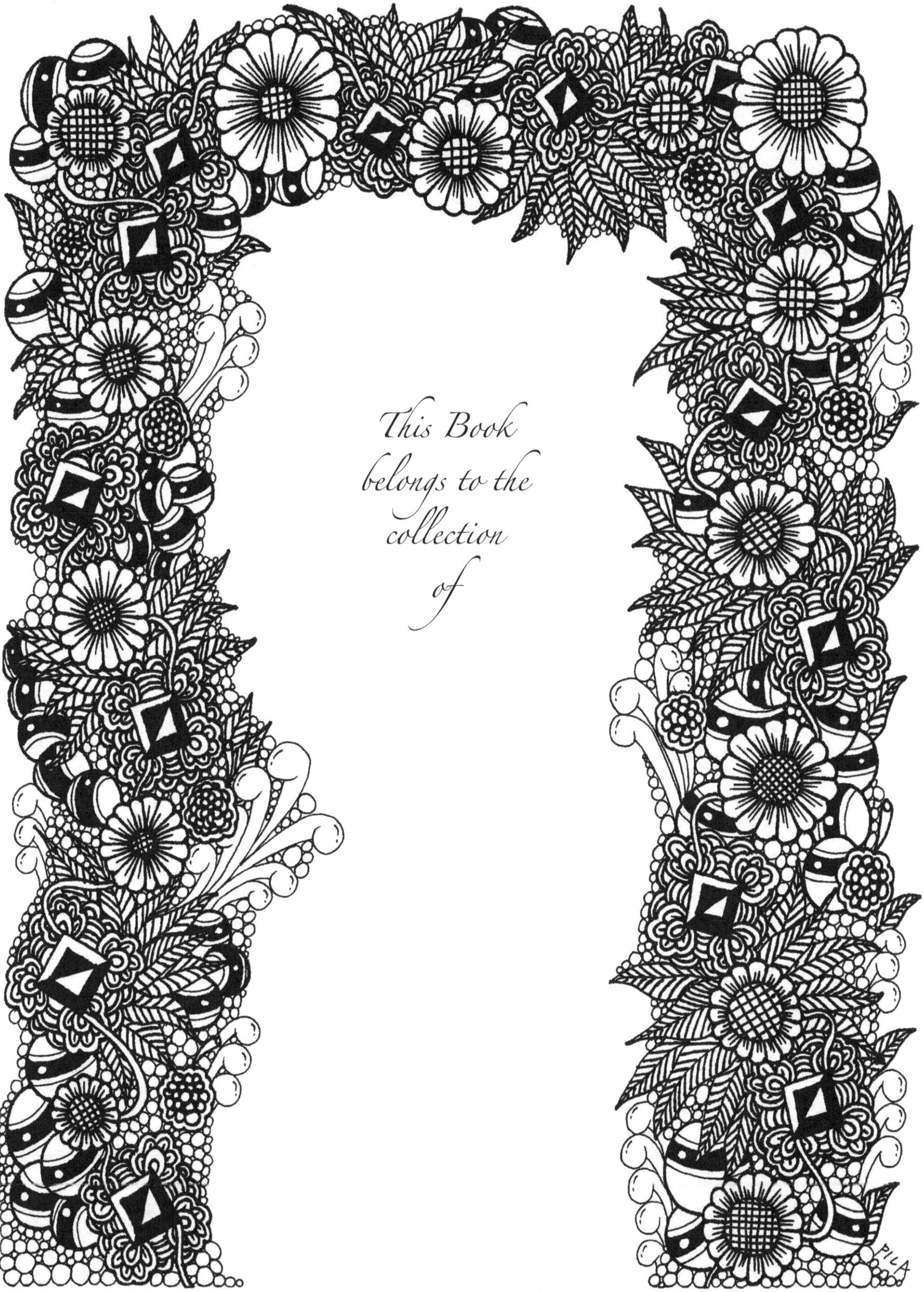


*This Book belongs to the collection of*

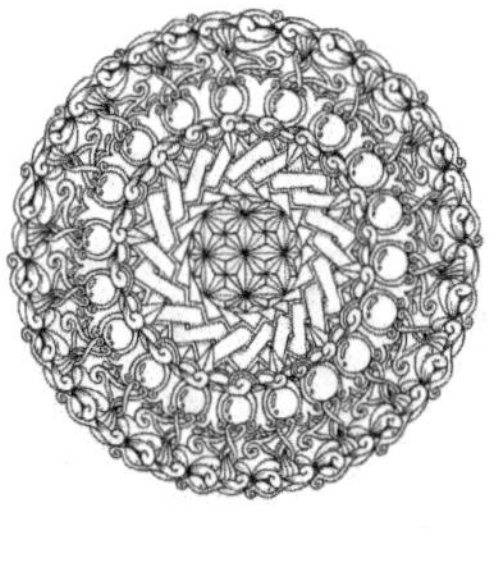
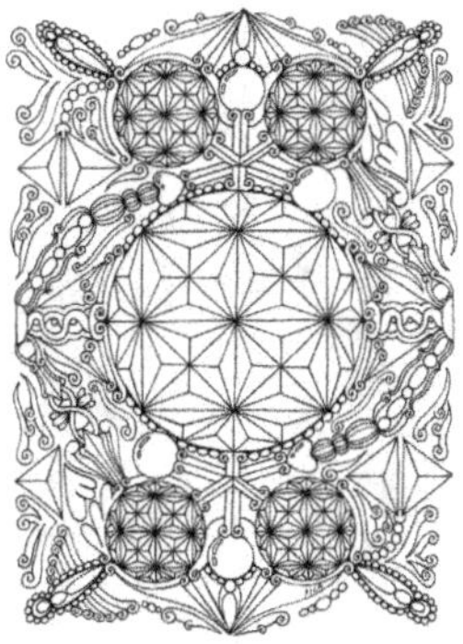
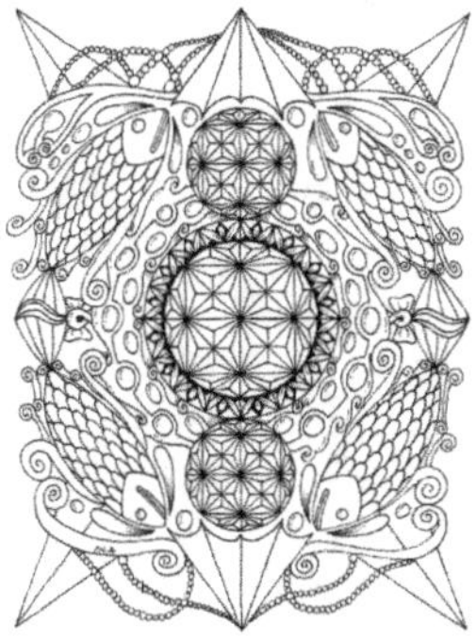
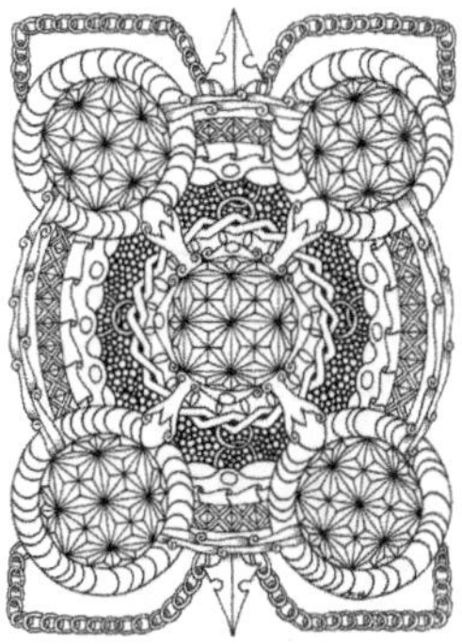
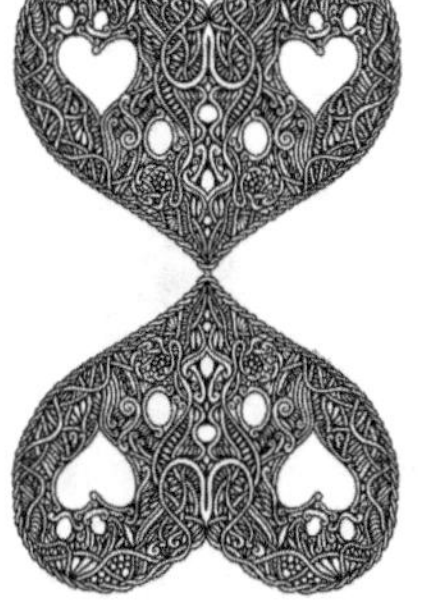
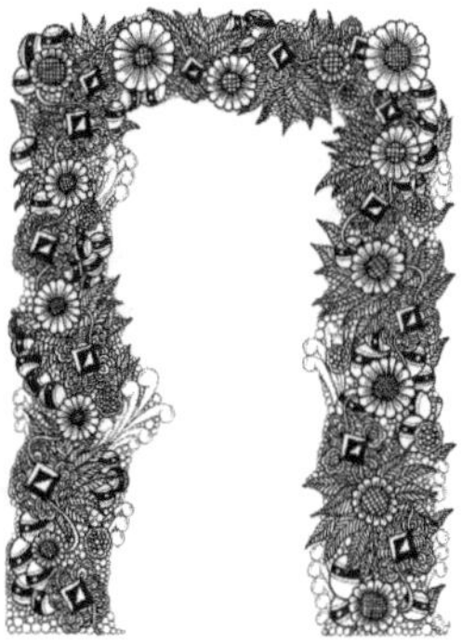
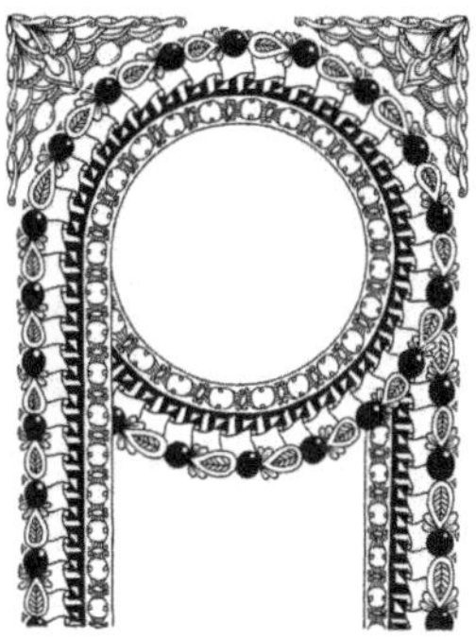
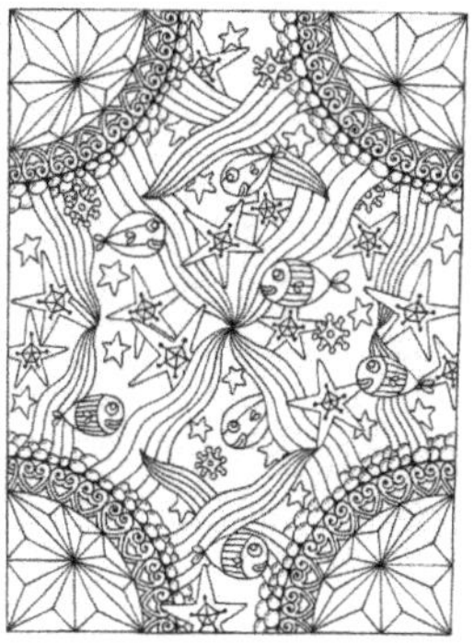
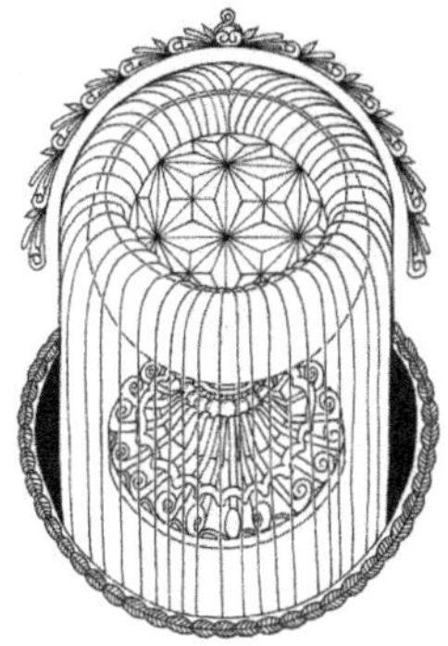
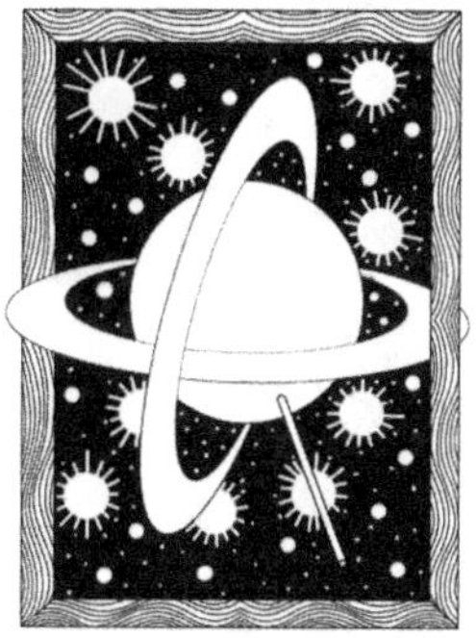
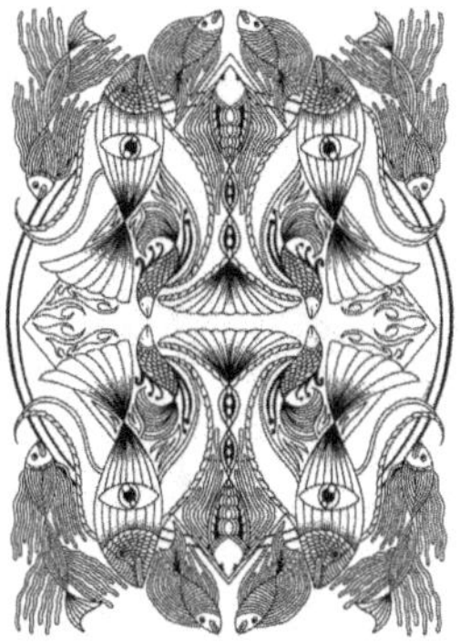
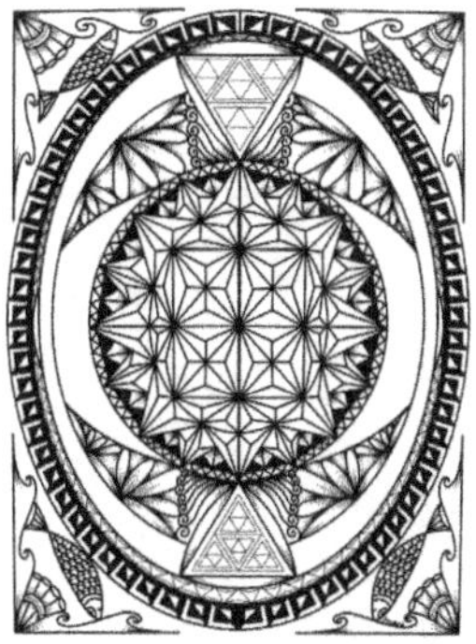
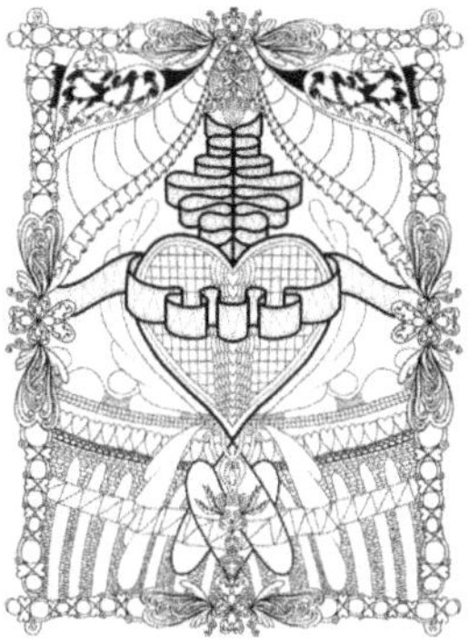
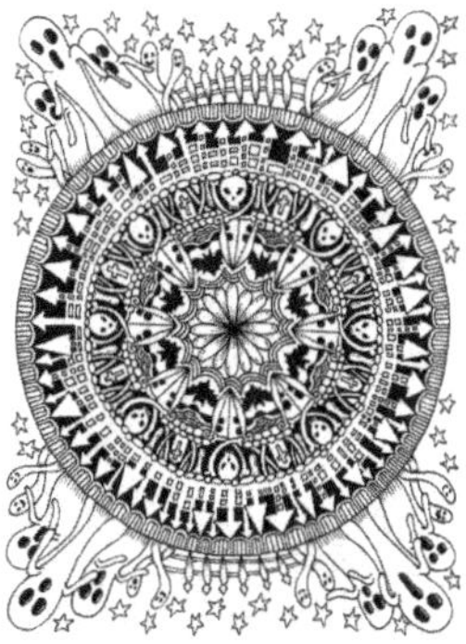
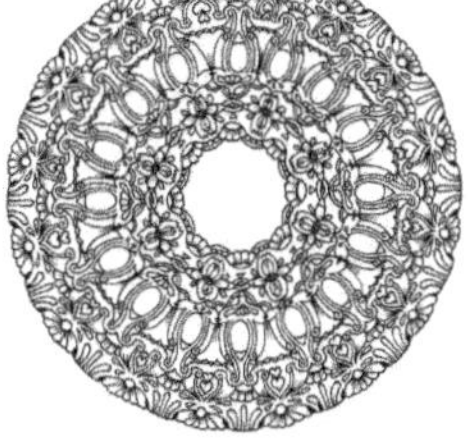
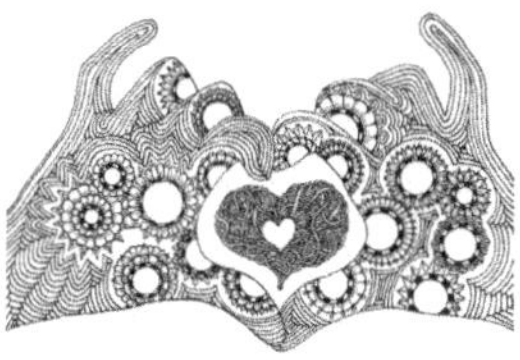
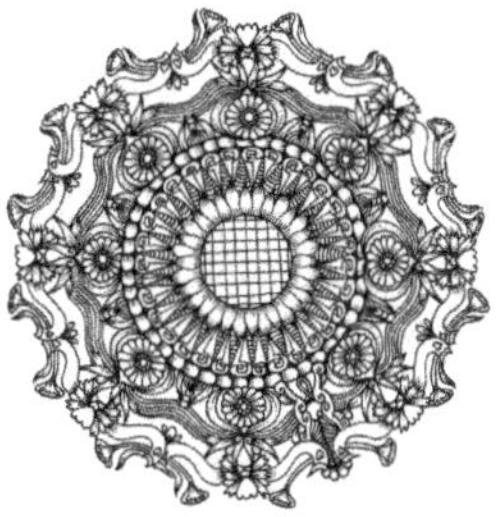
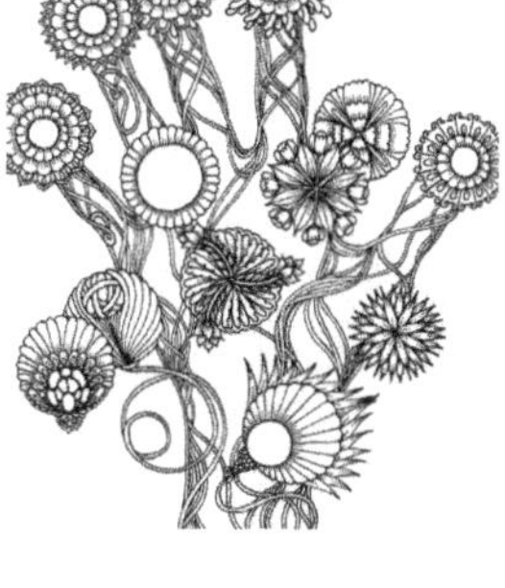
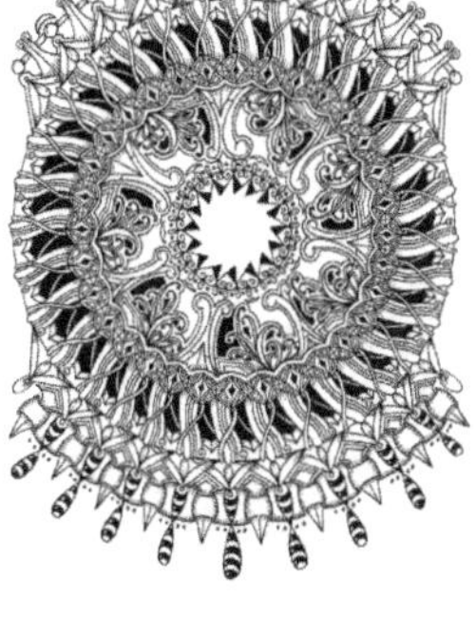
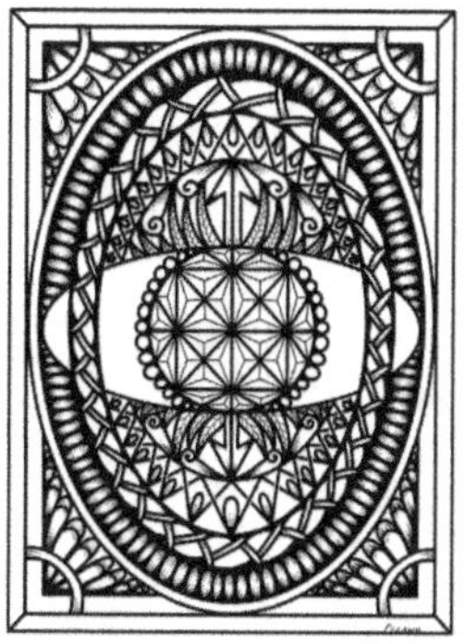
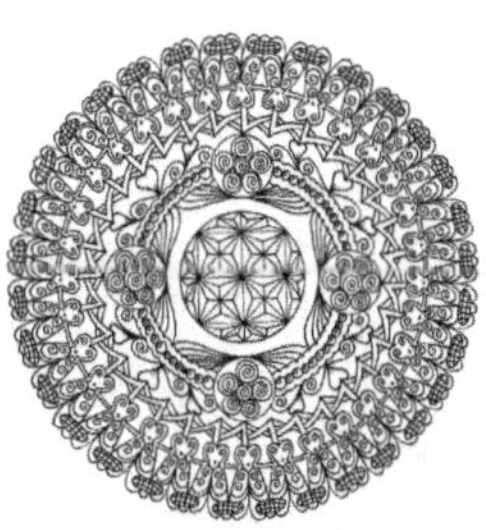
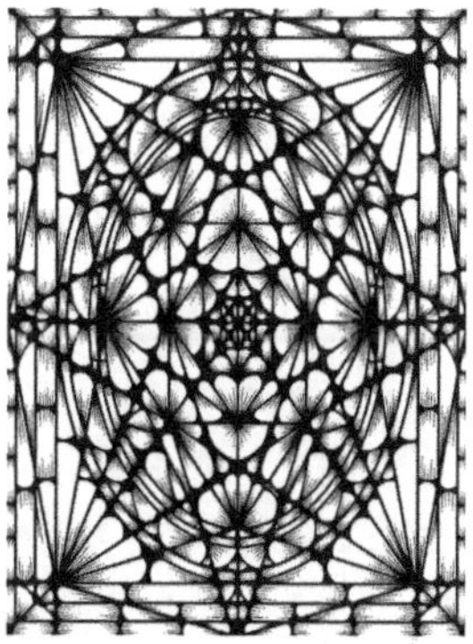
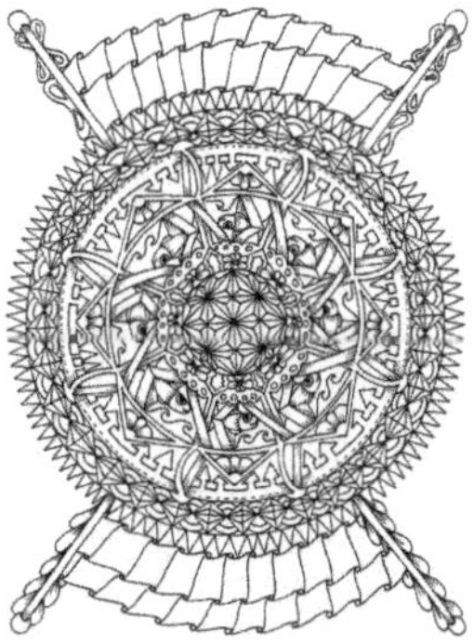
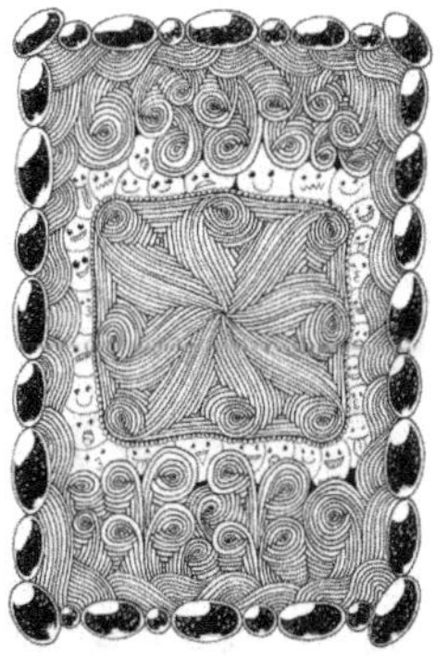
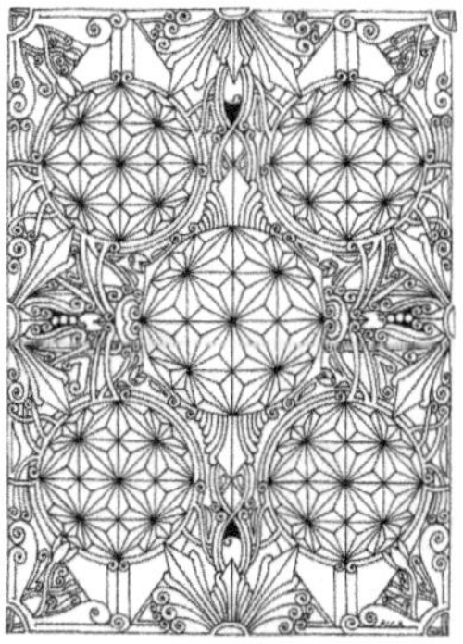

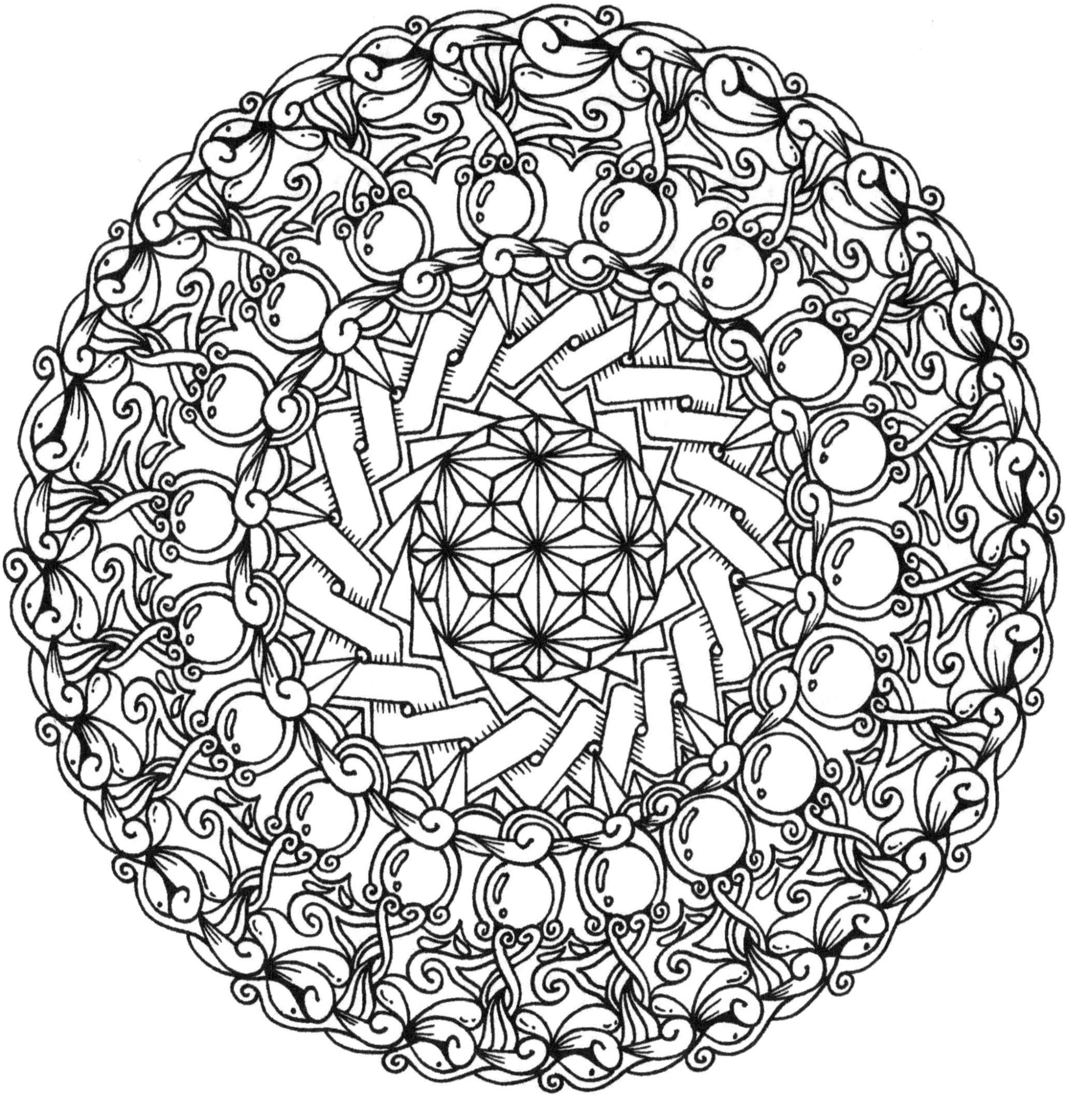

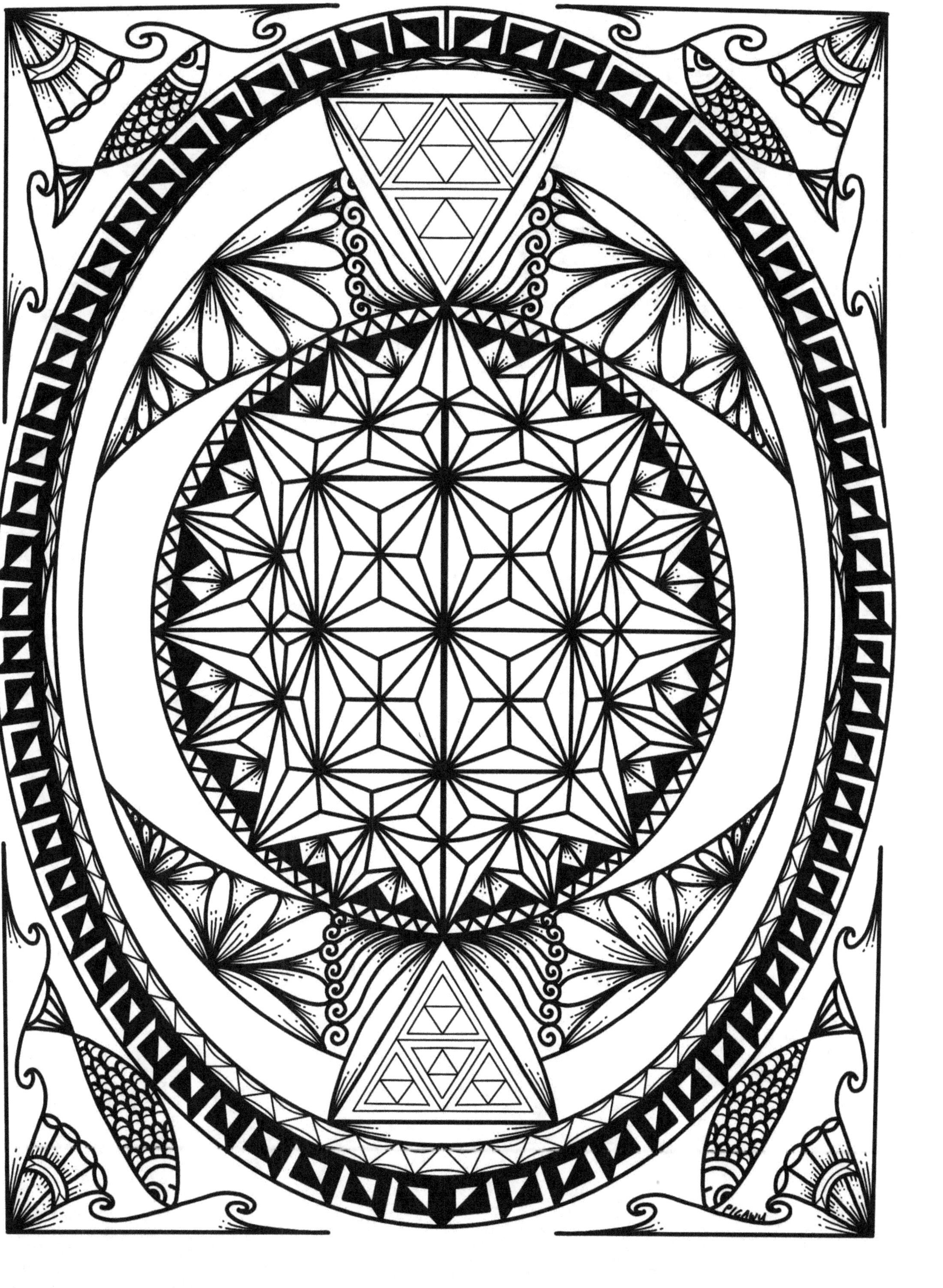
PIGANU

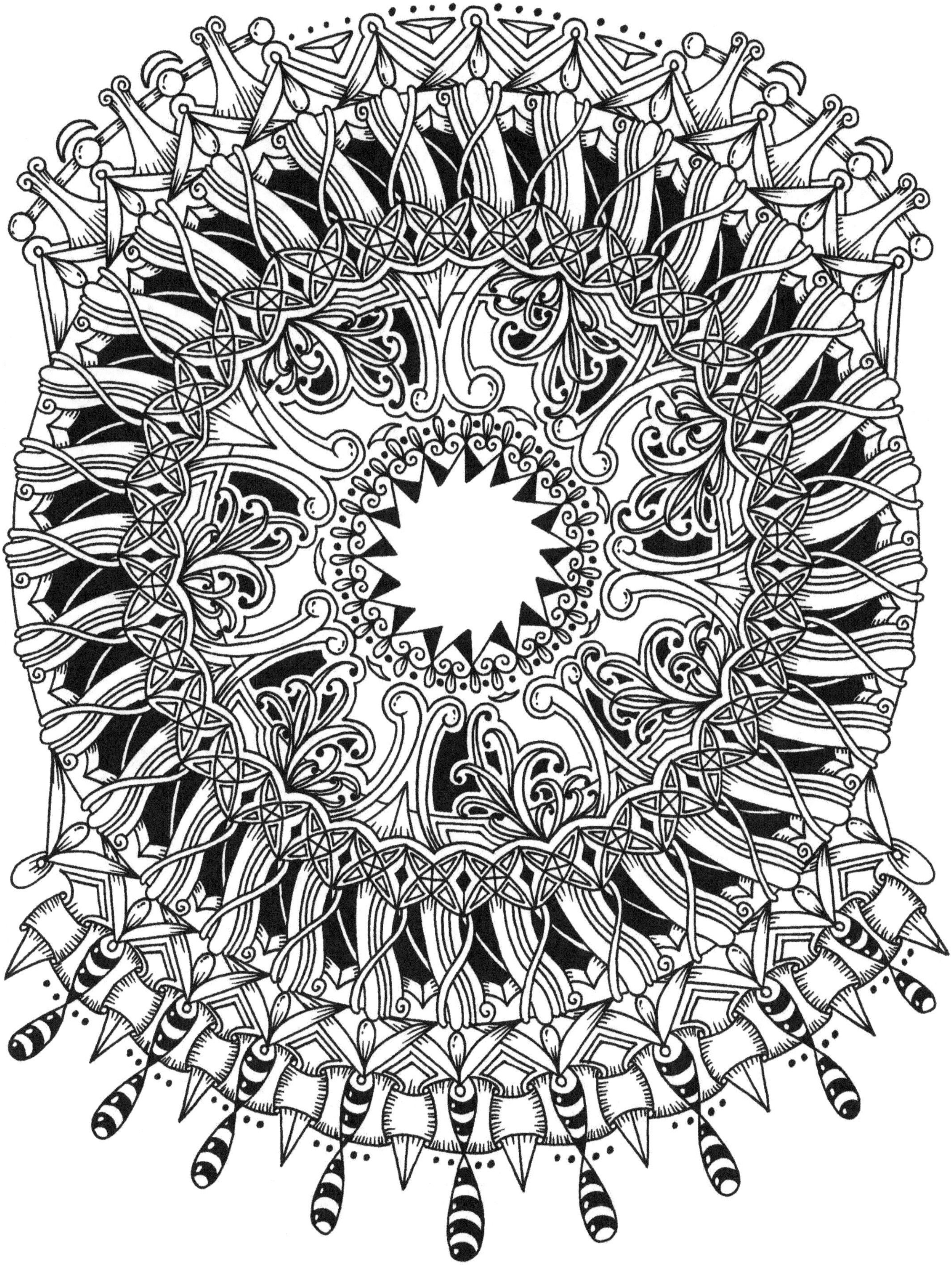

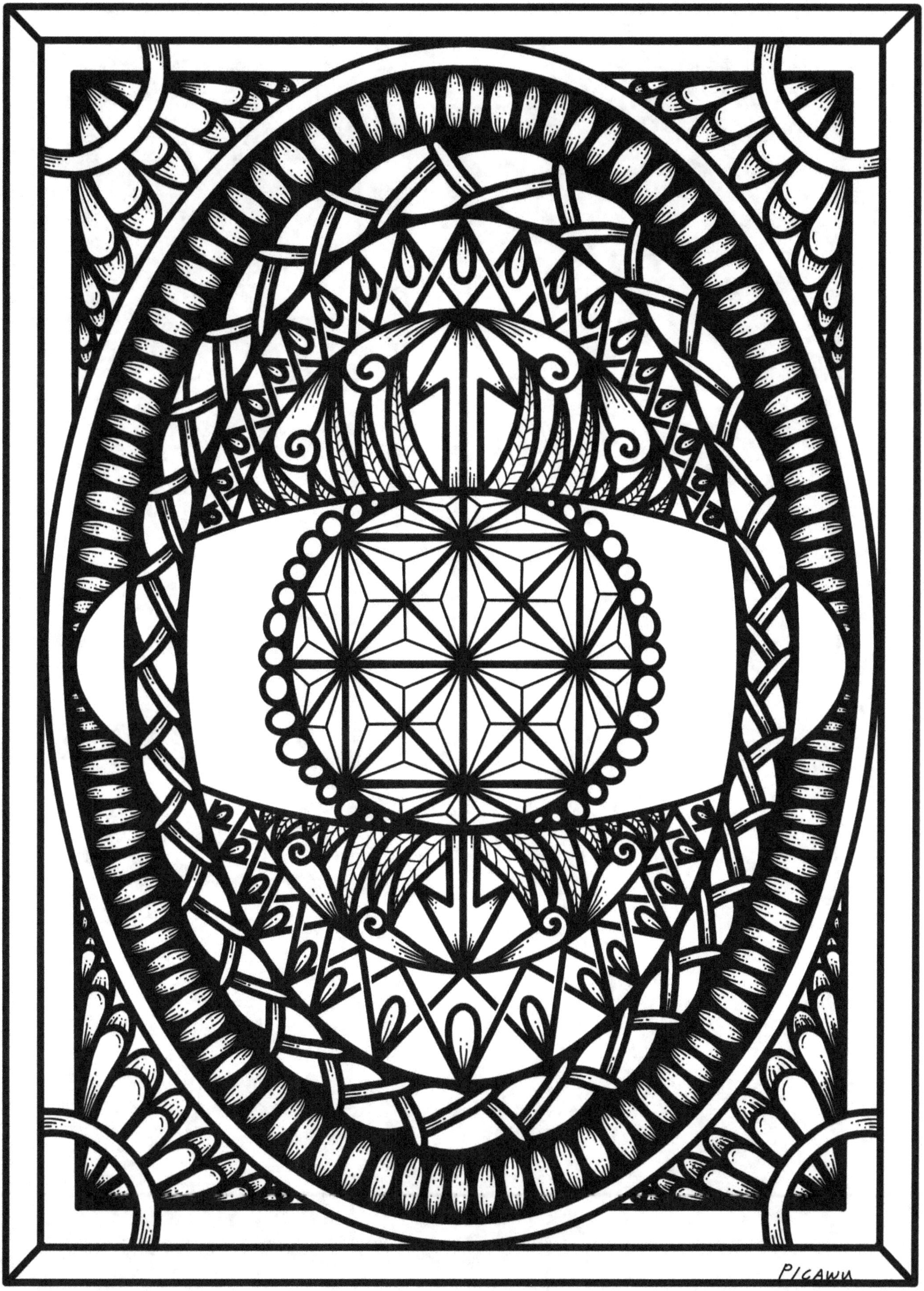
PICAWU

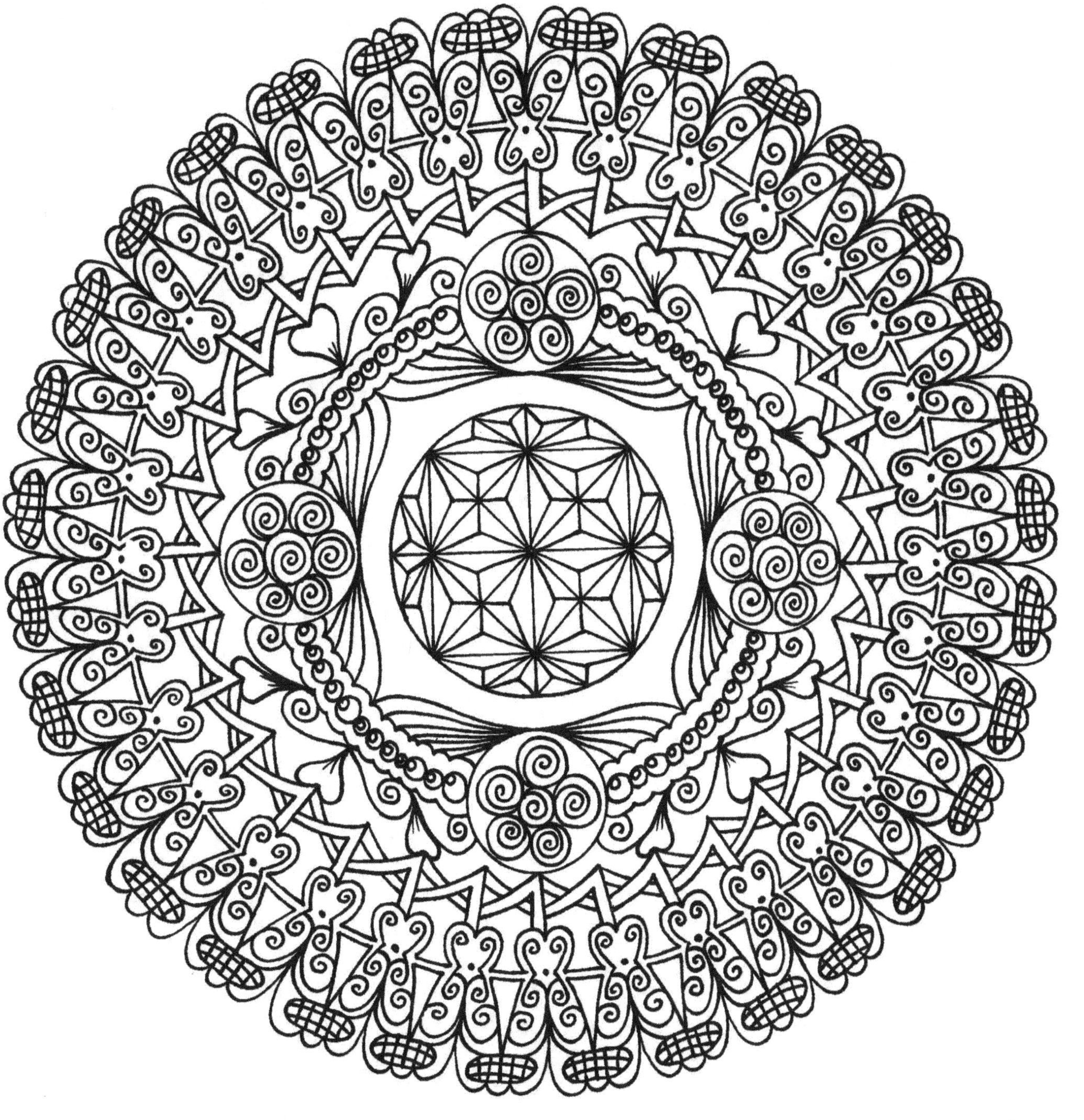

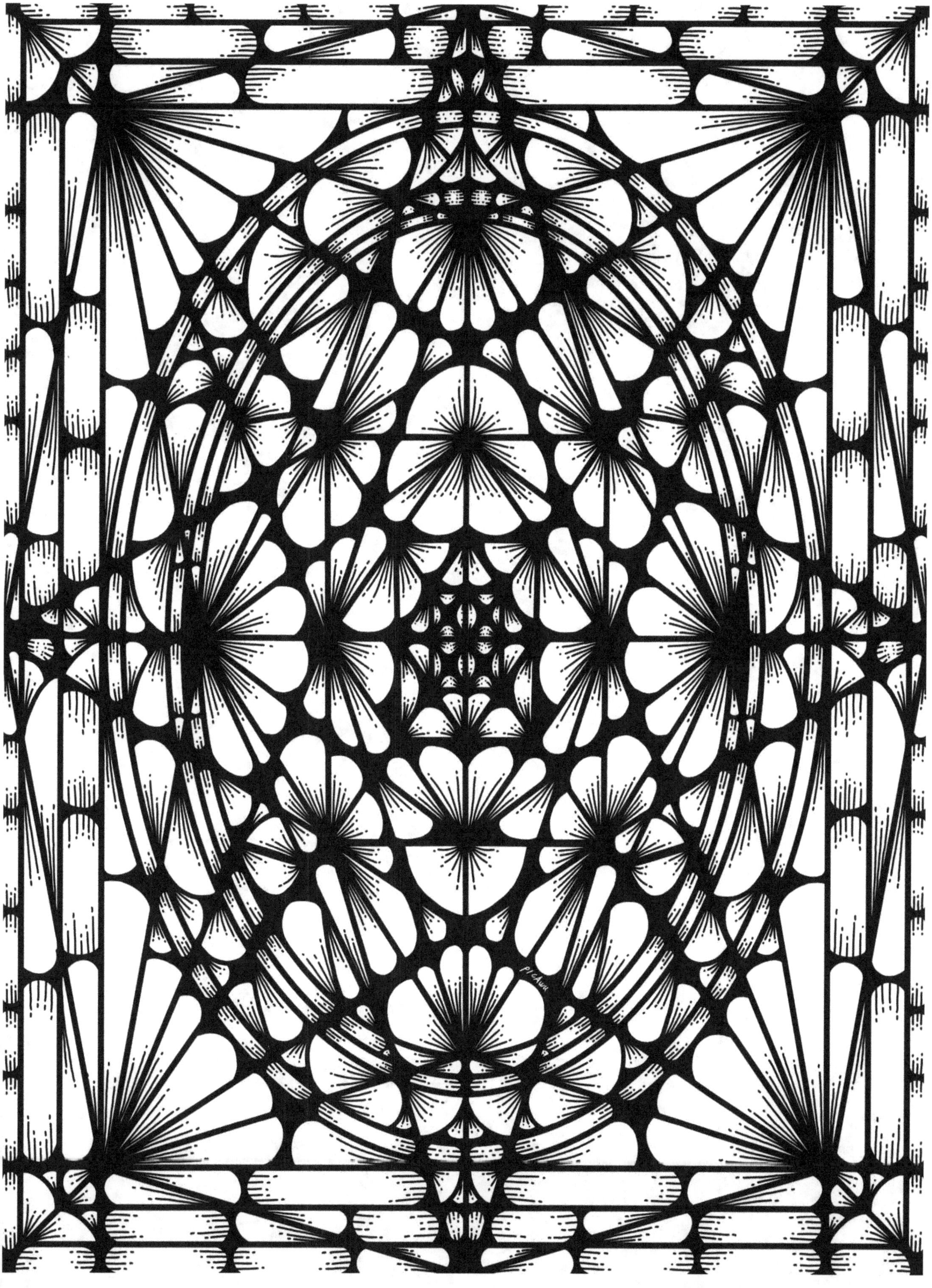

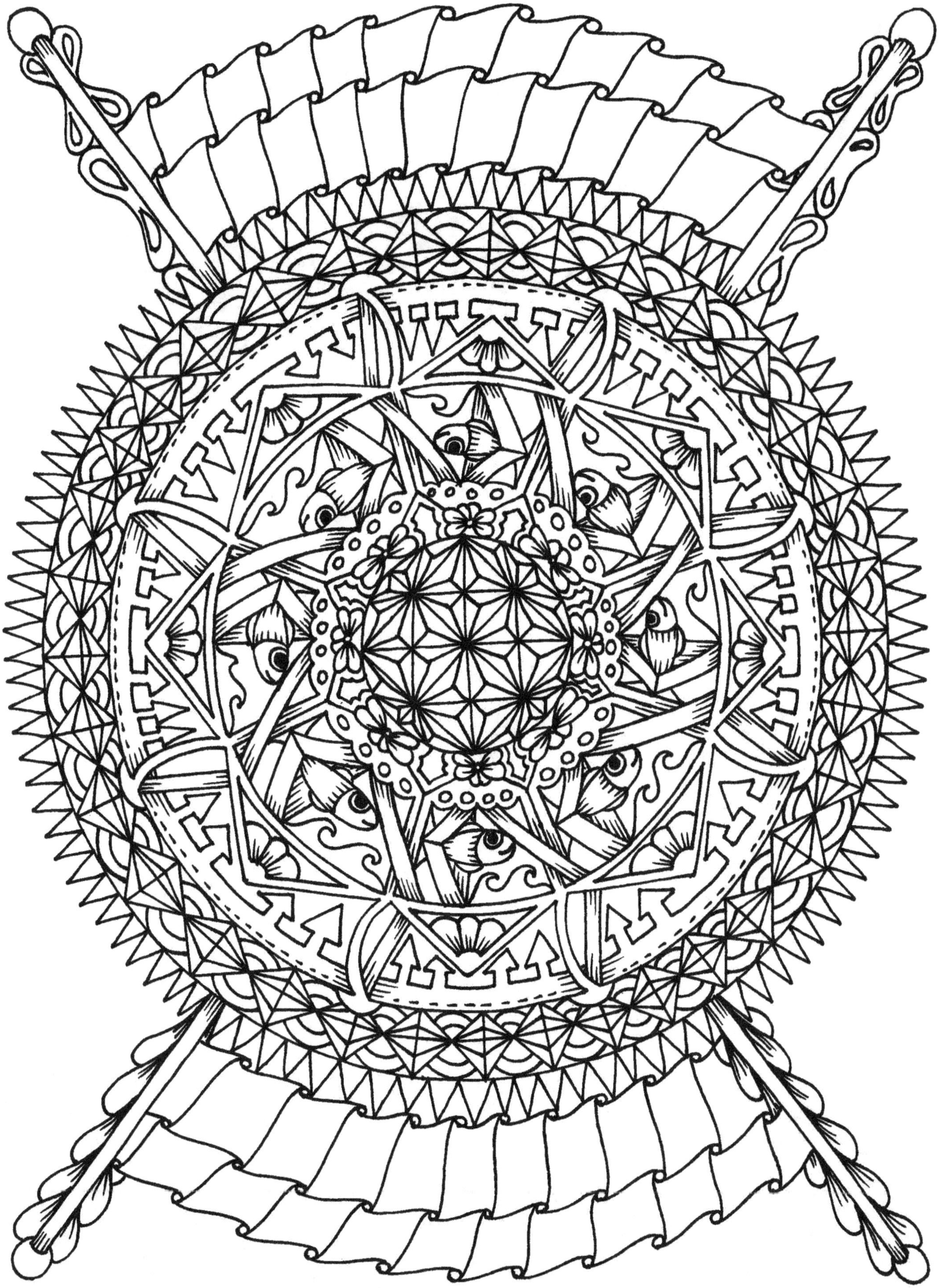

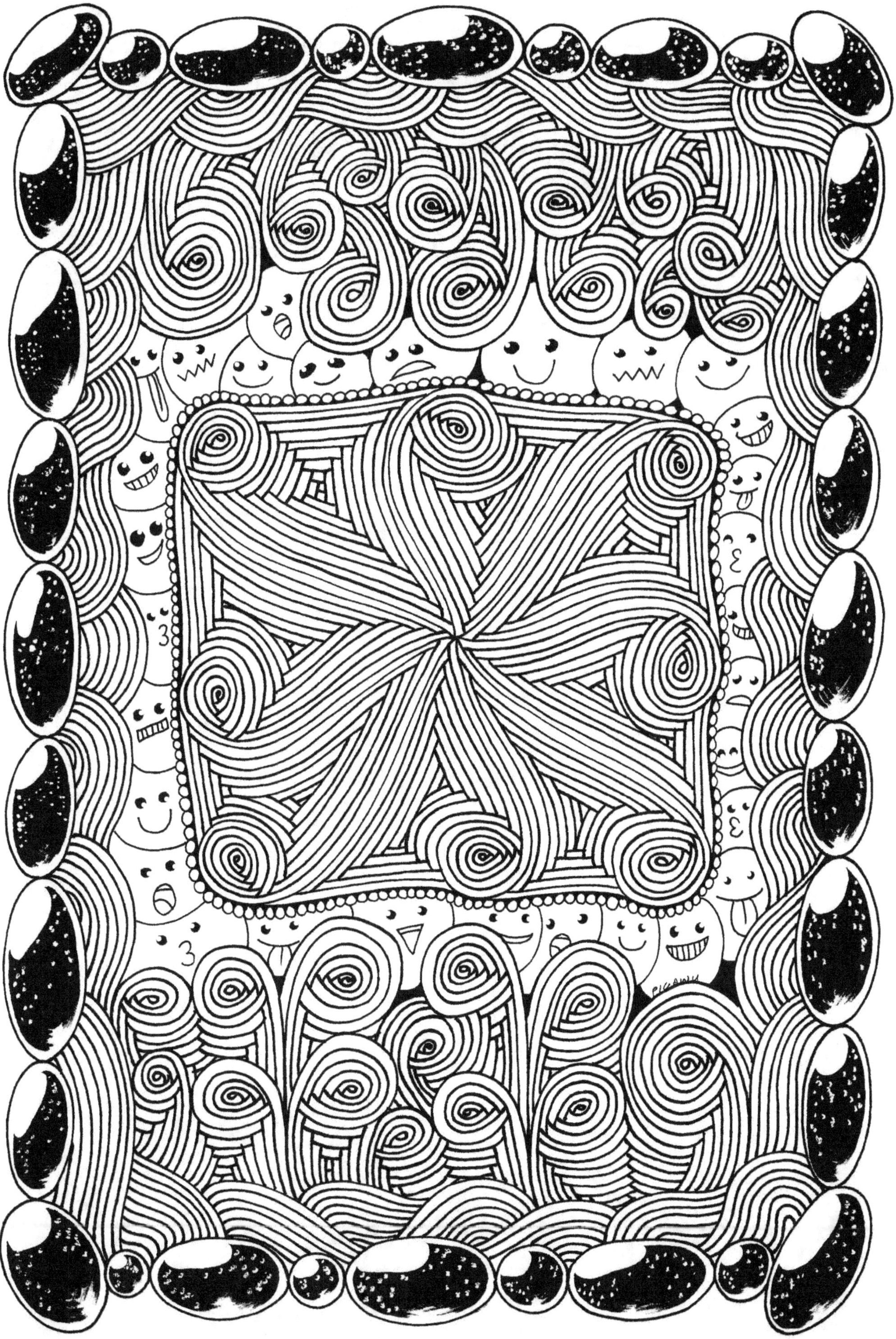

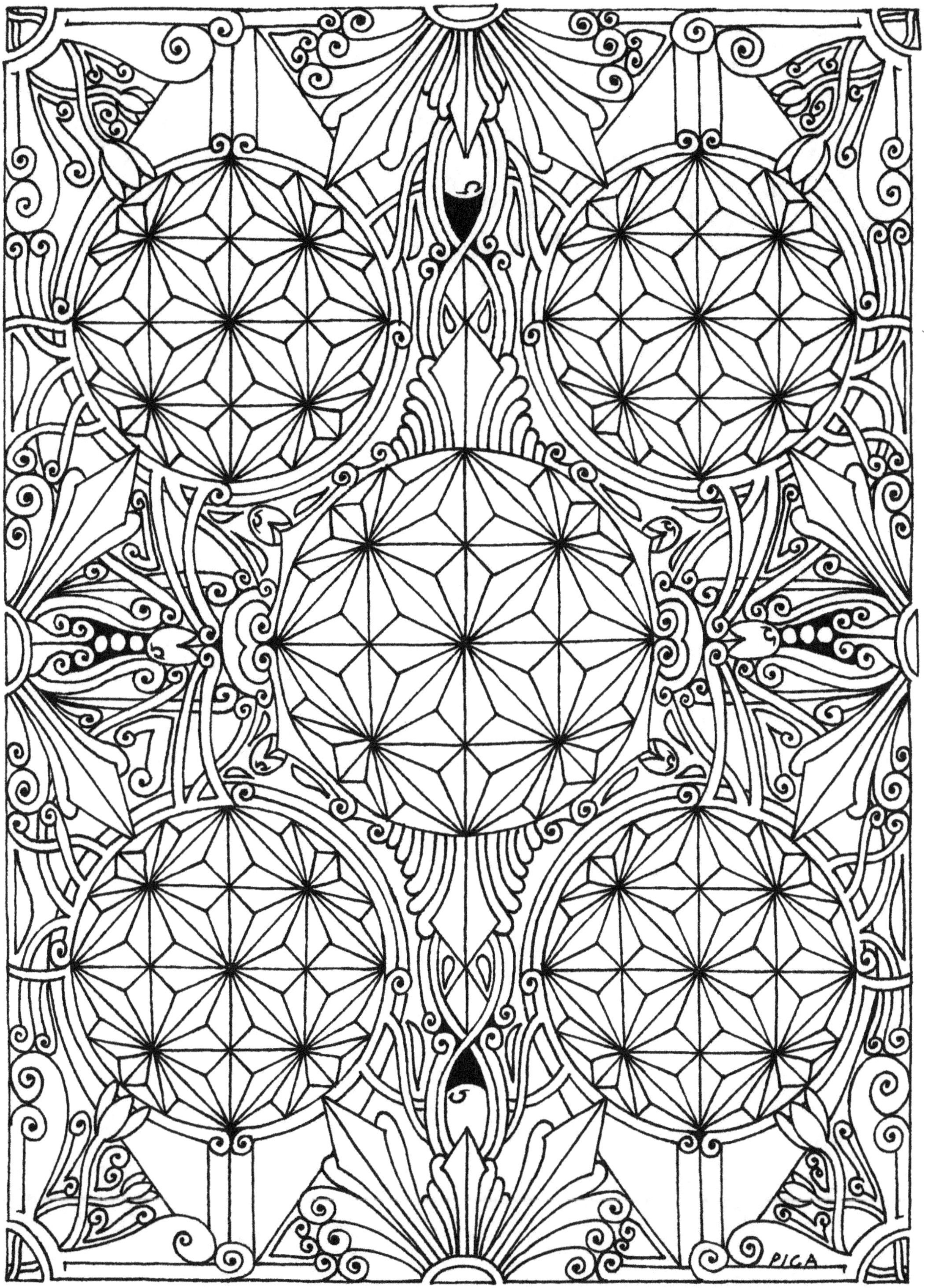
PIGA

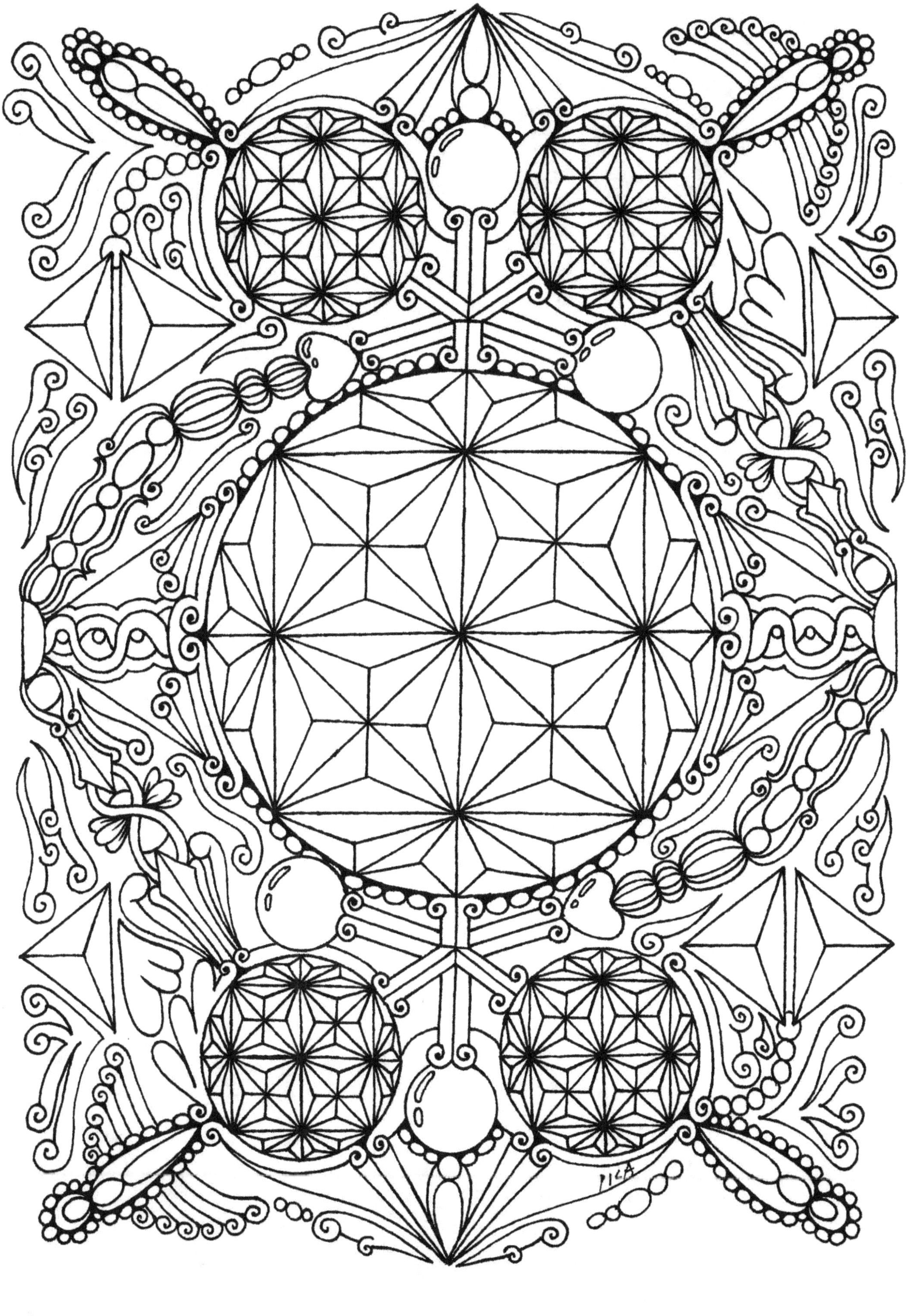

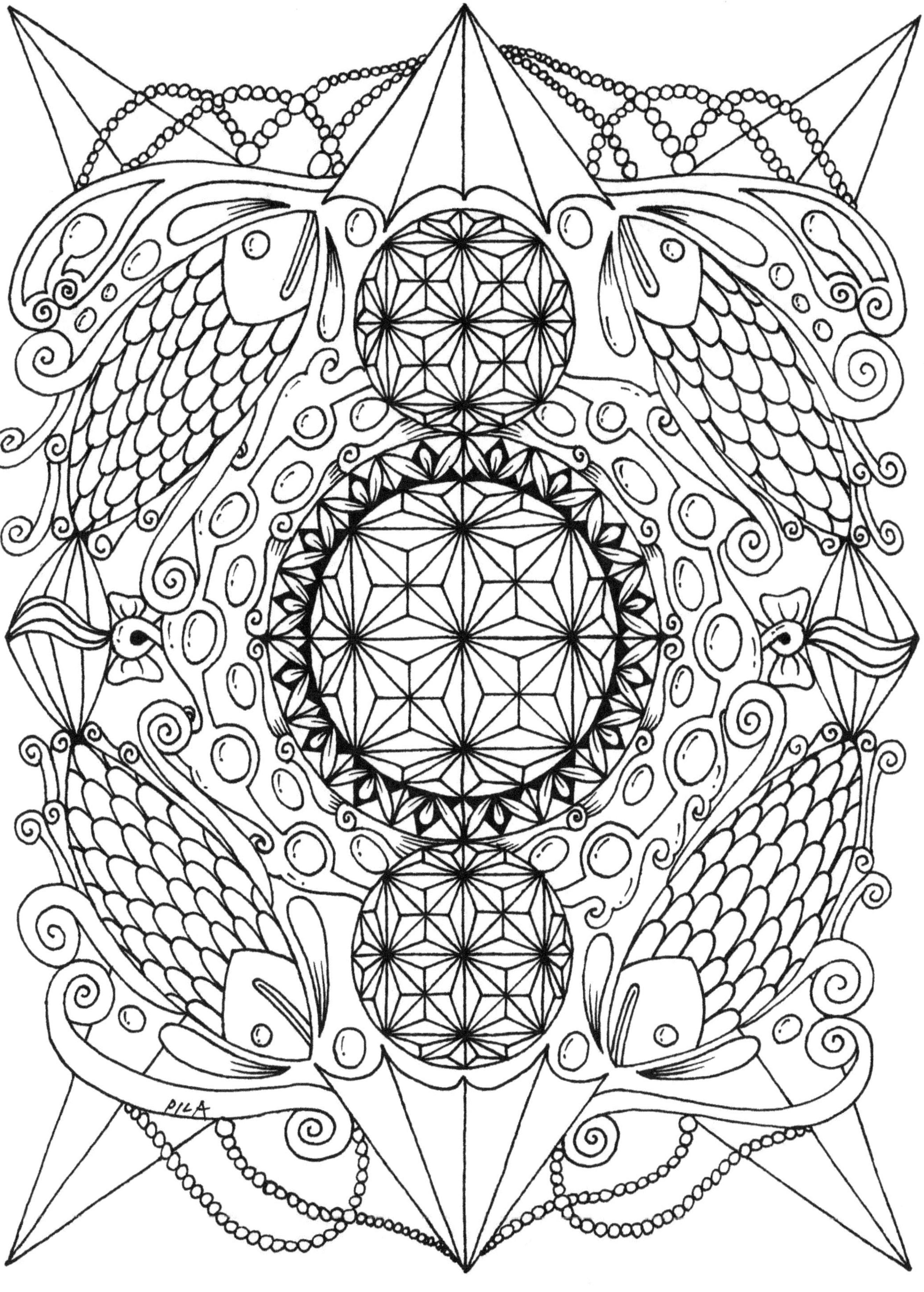
PILA

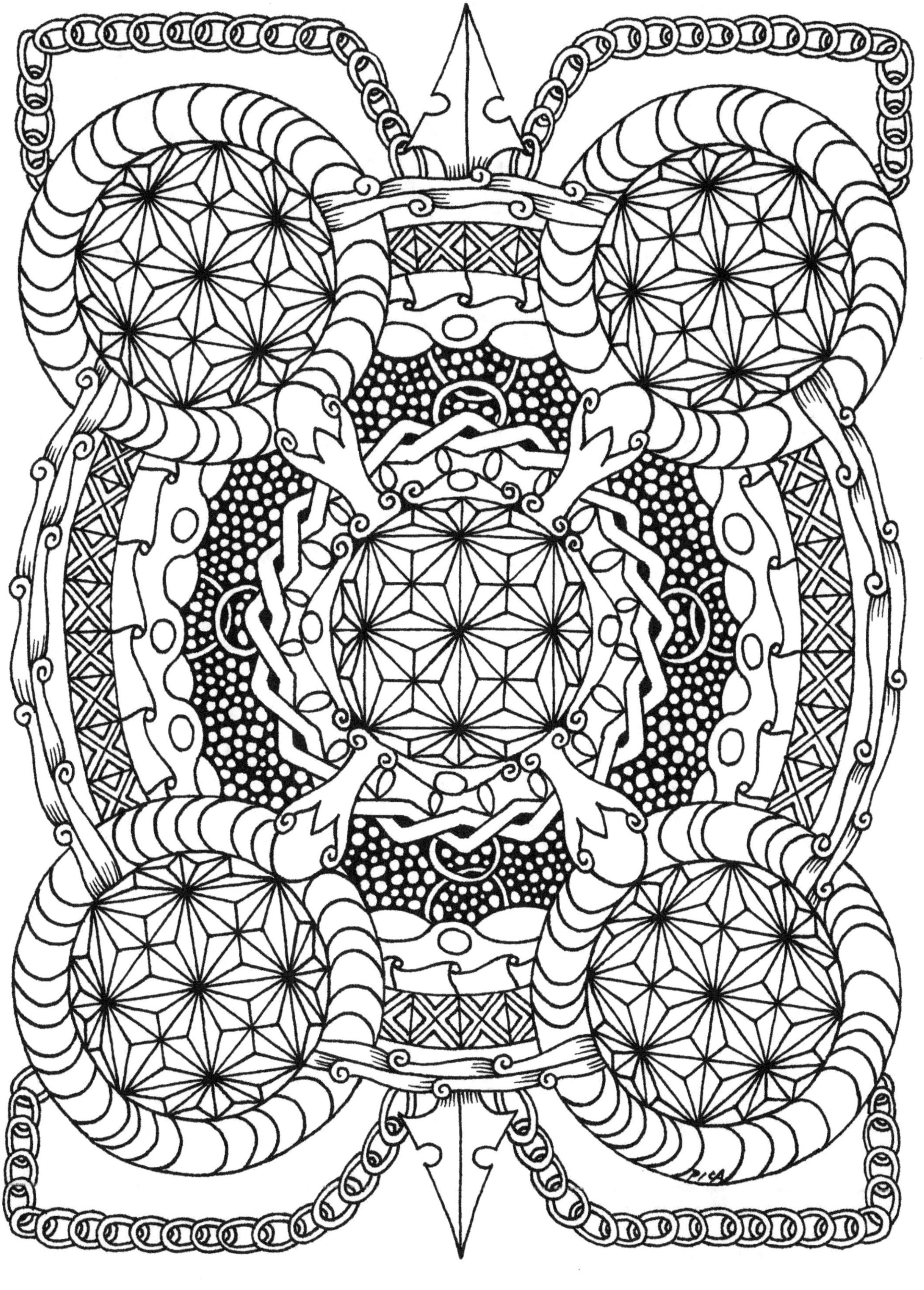

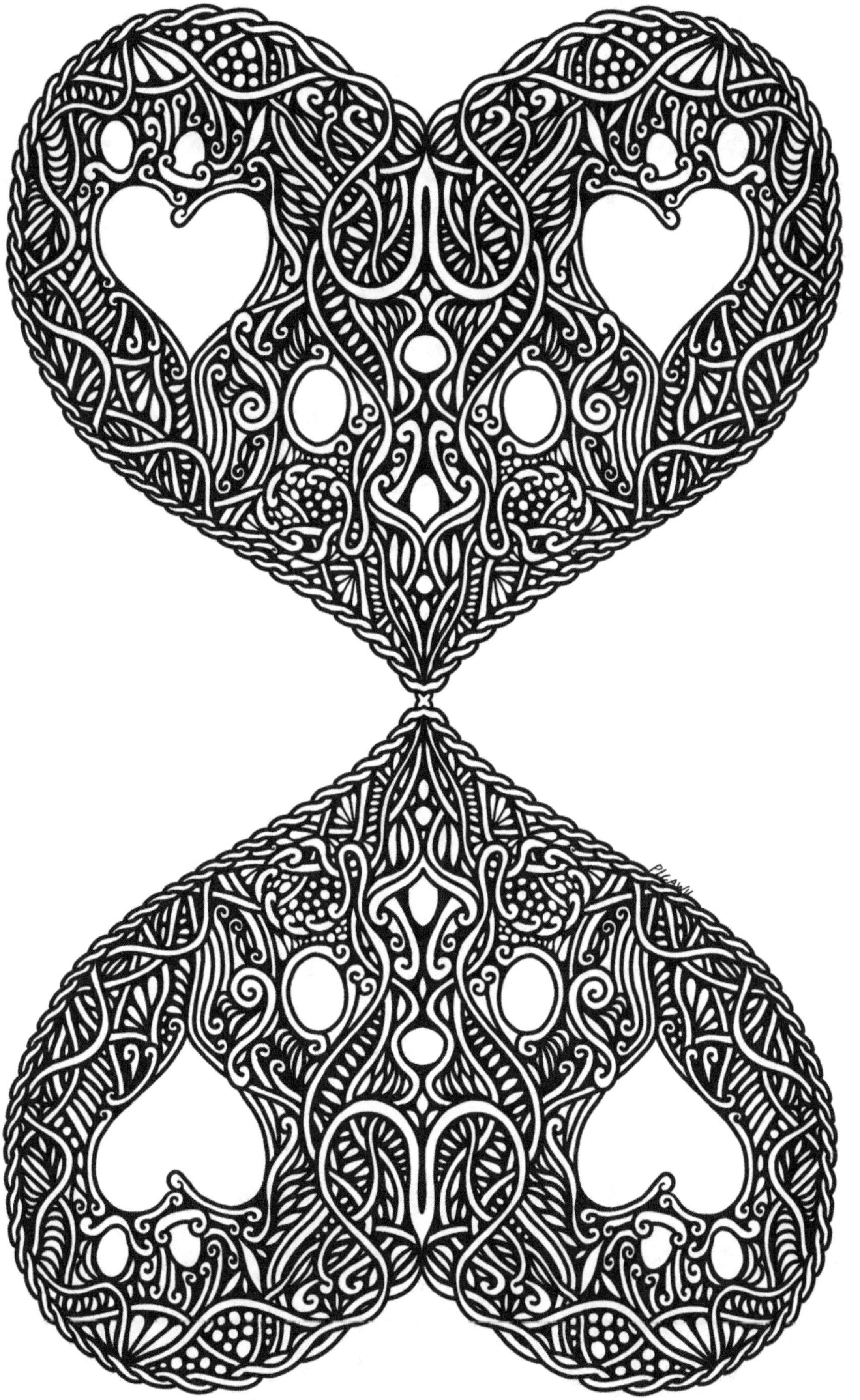

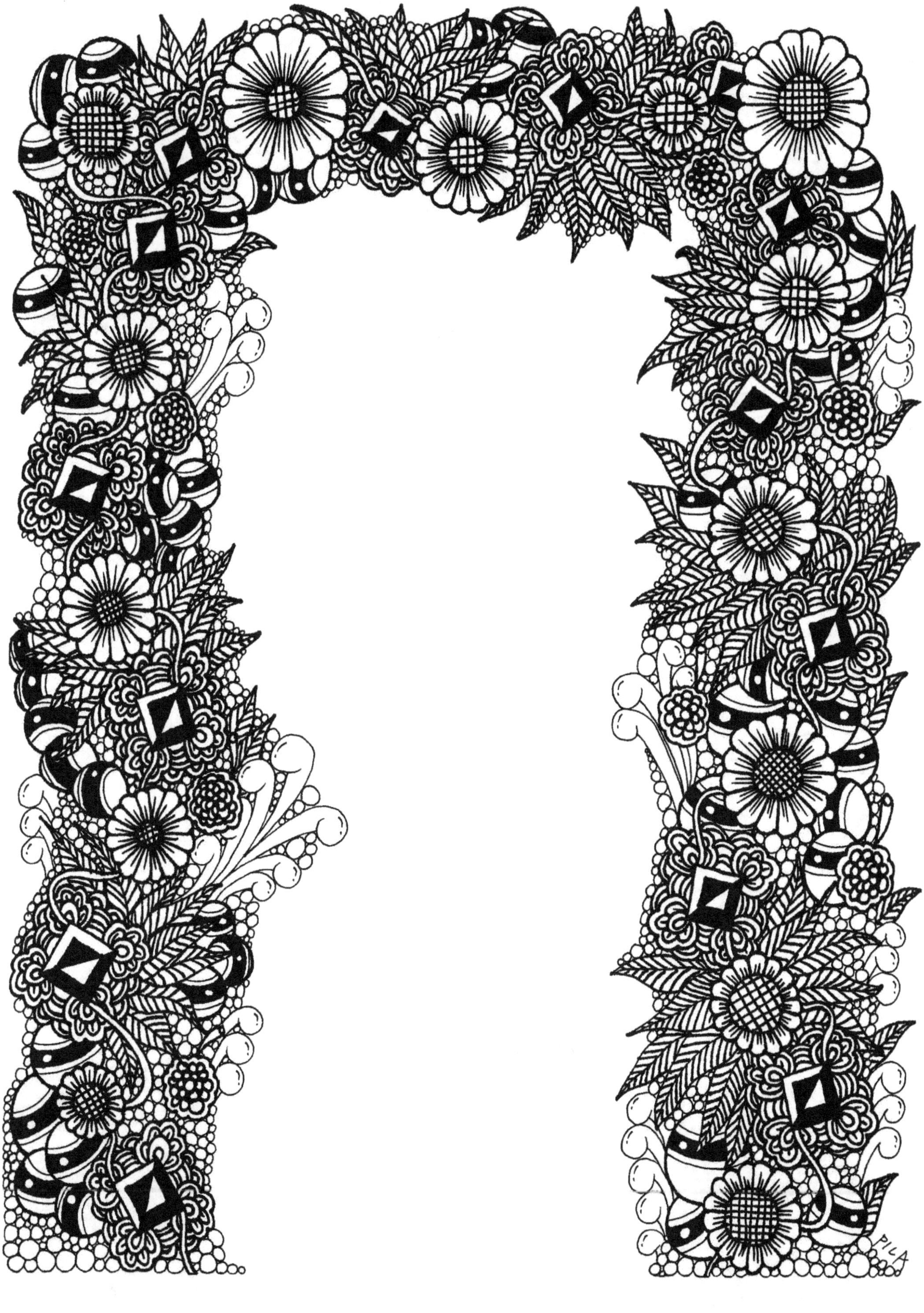
PILA

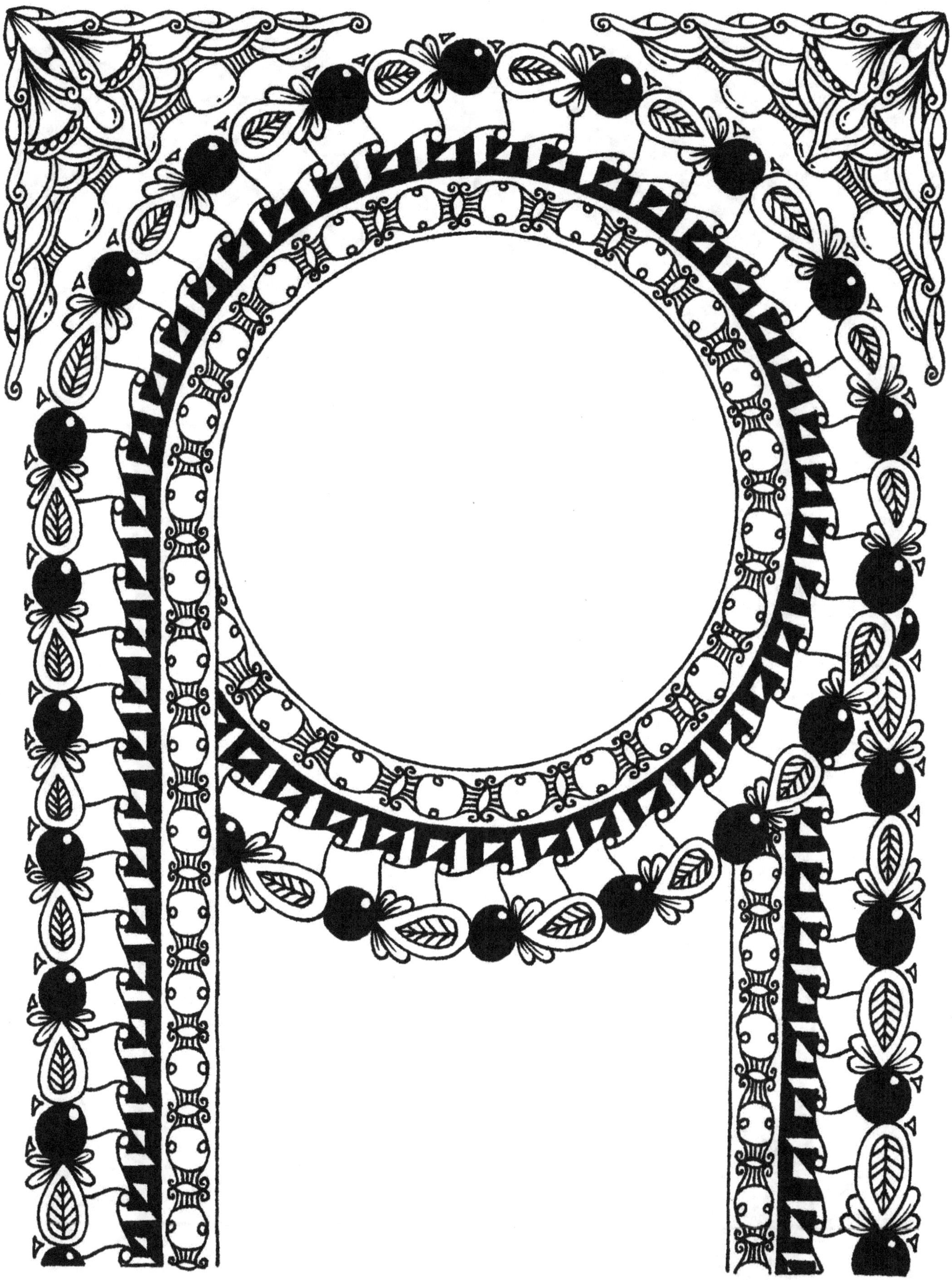

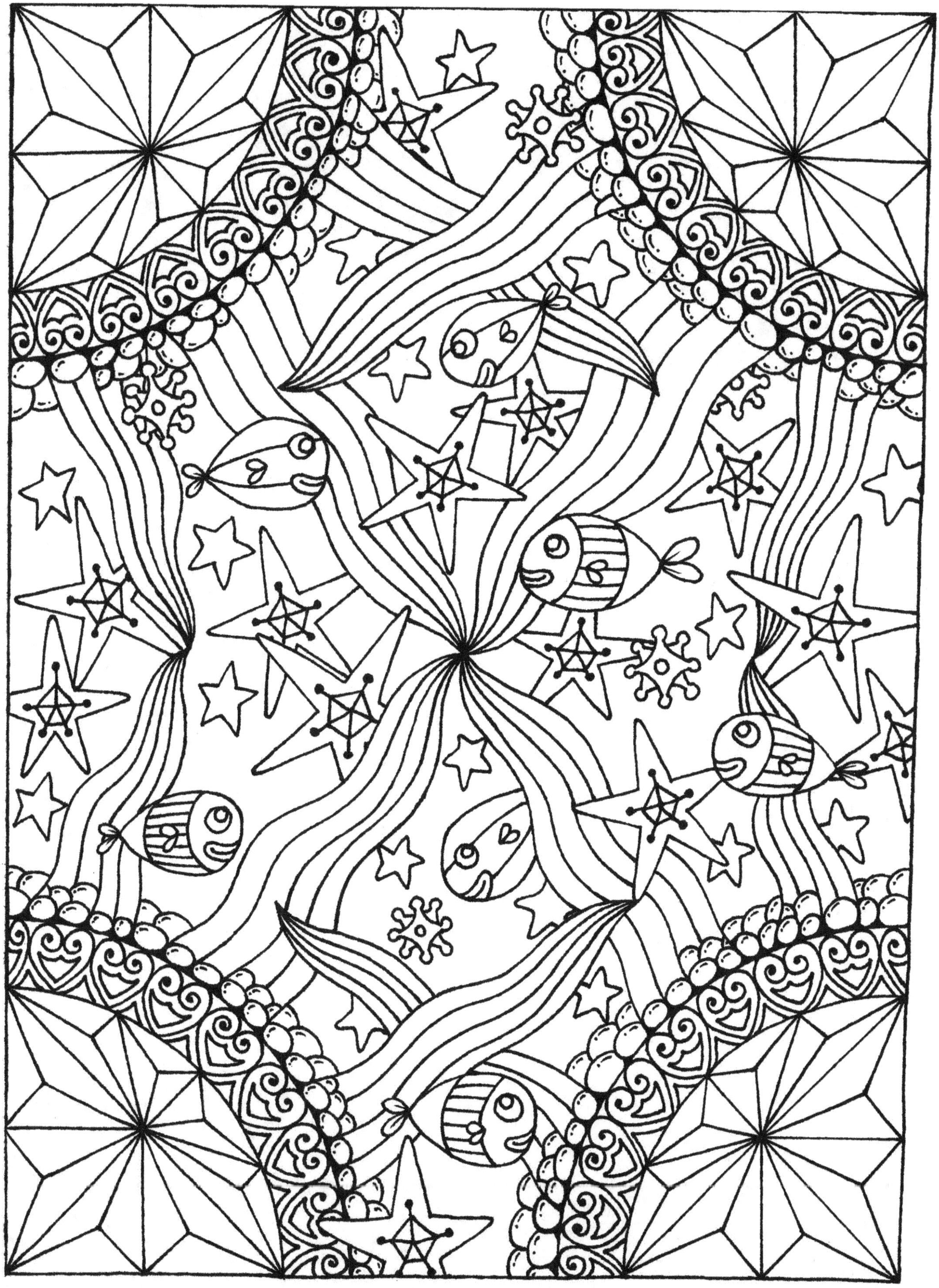

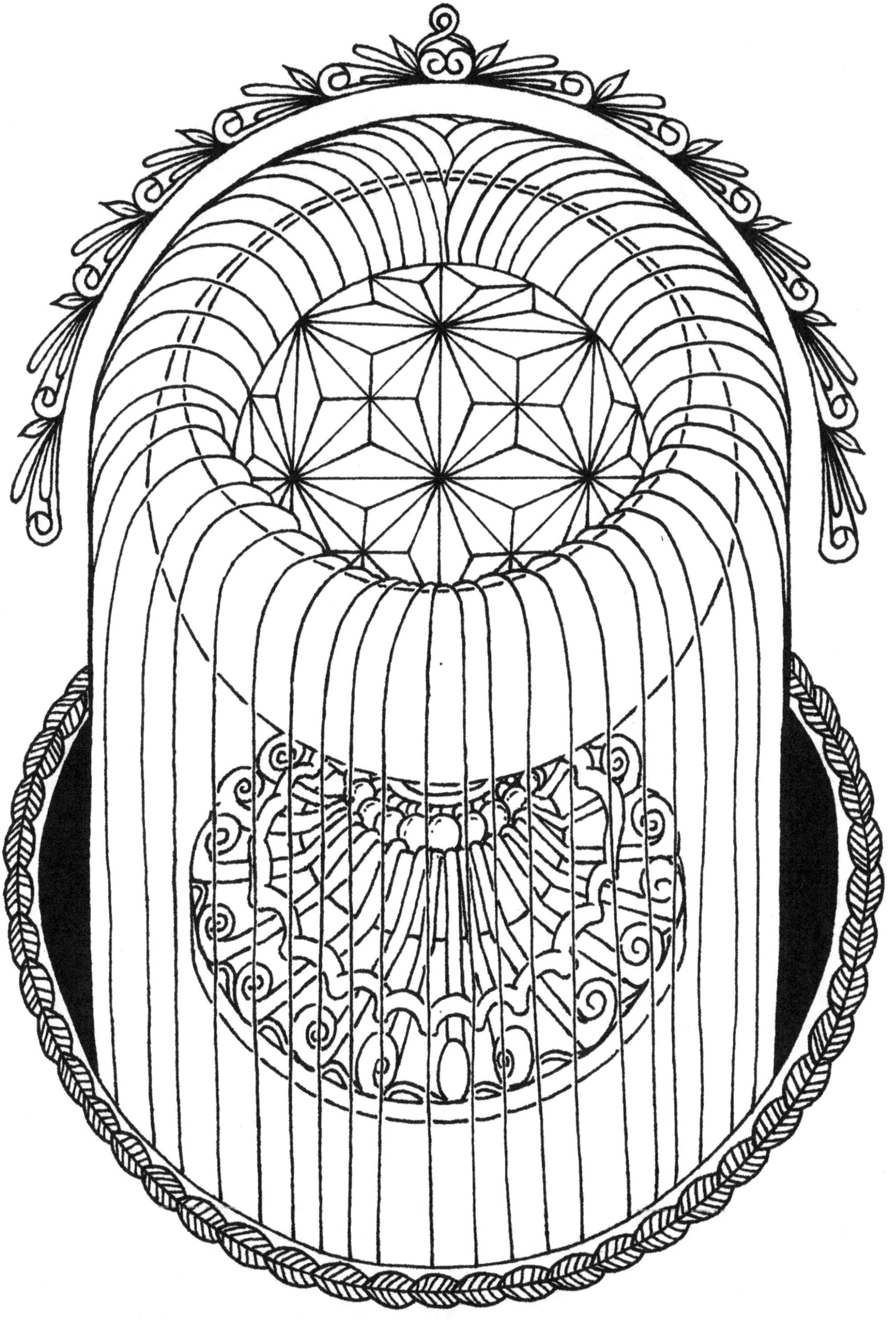

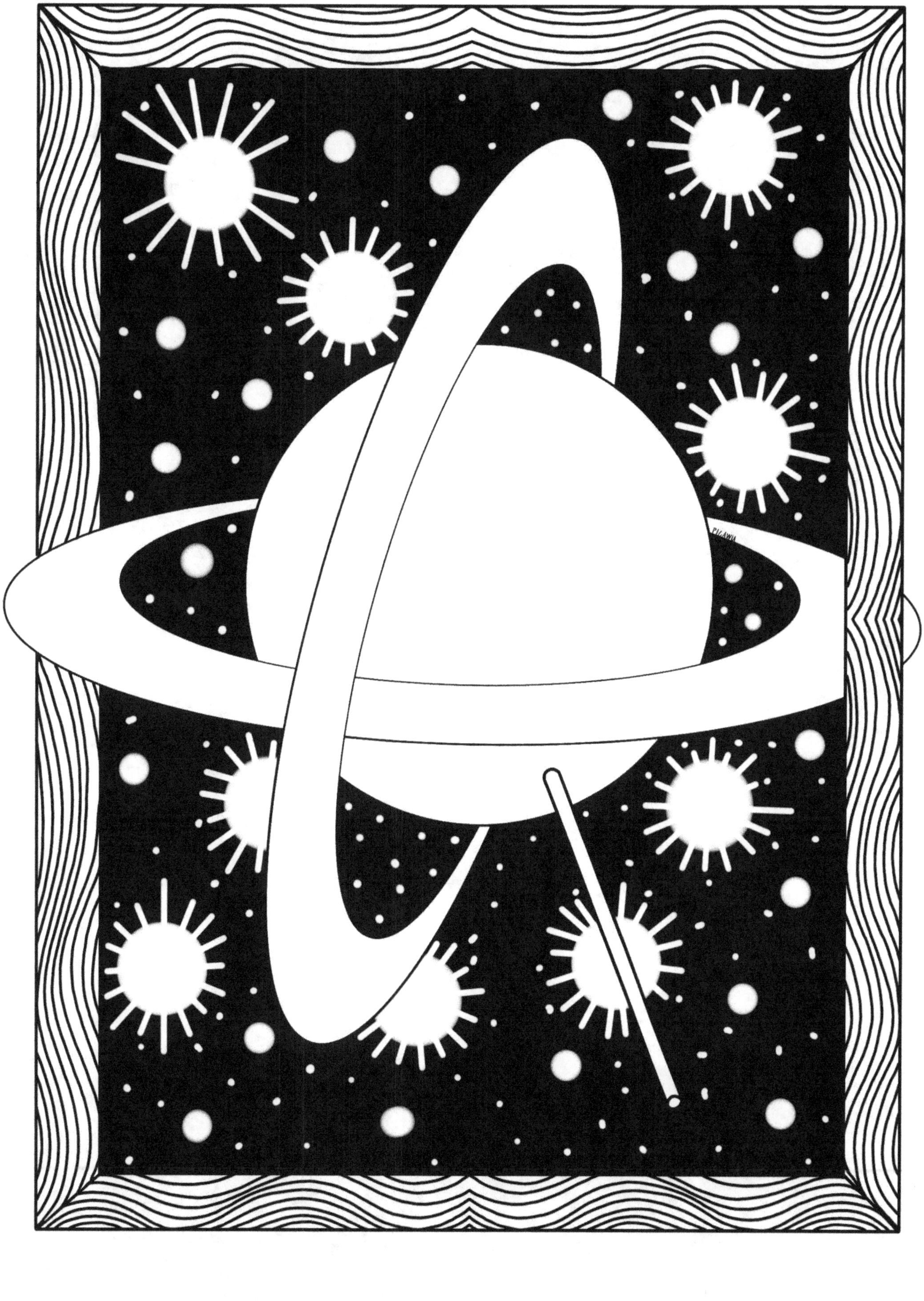

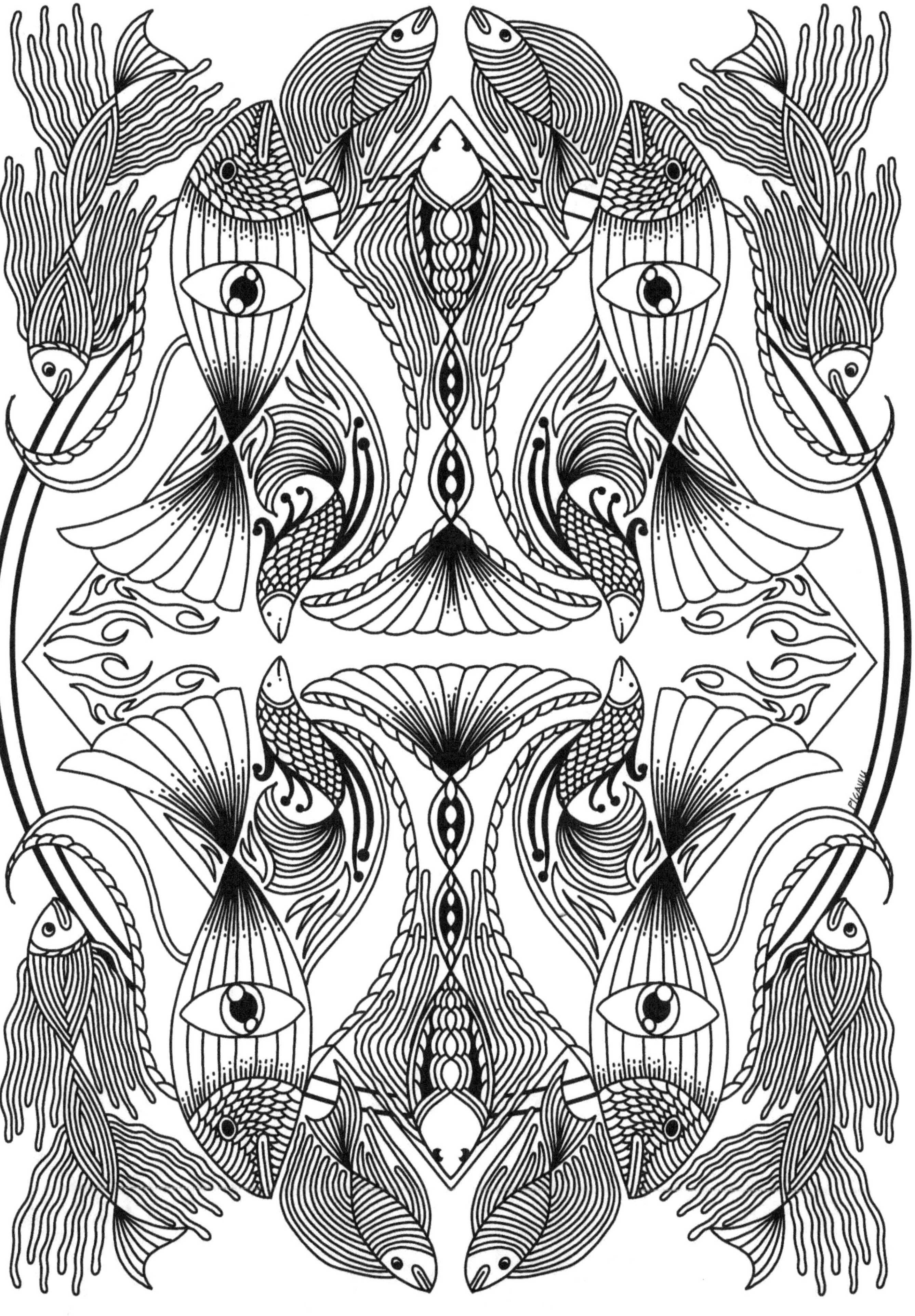

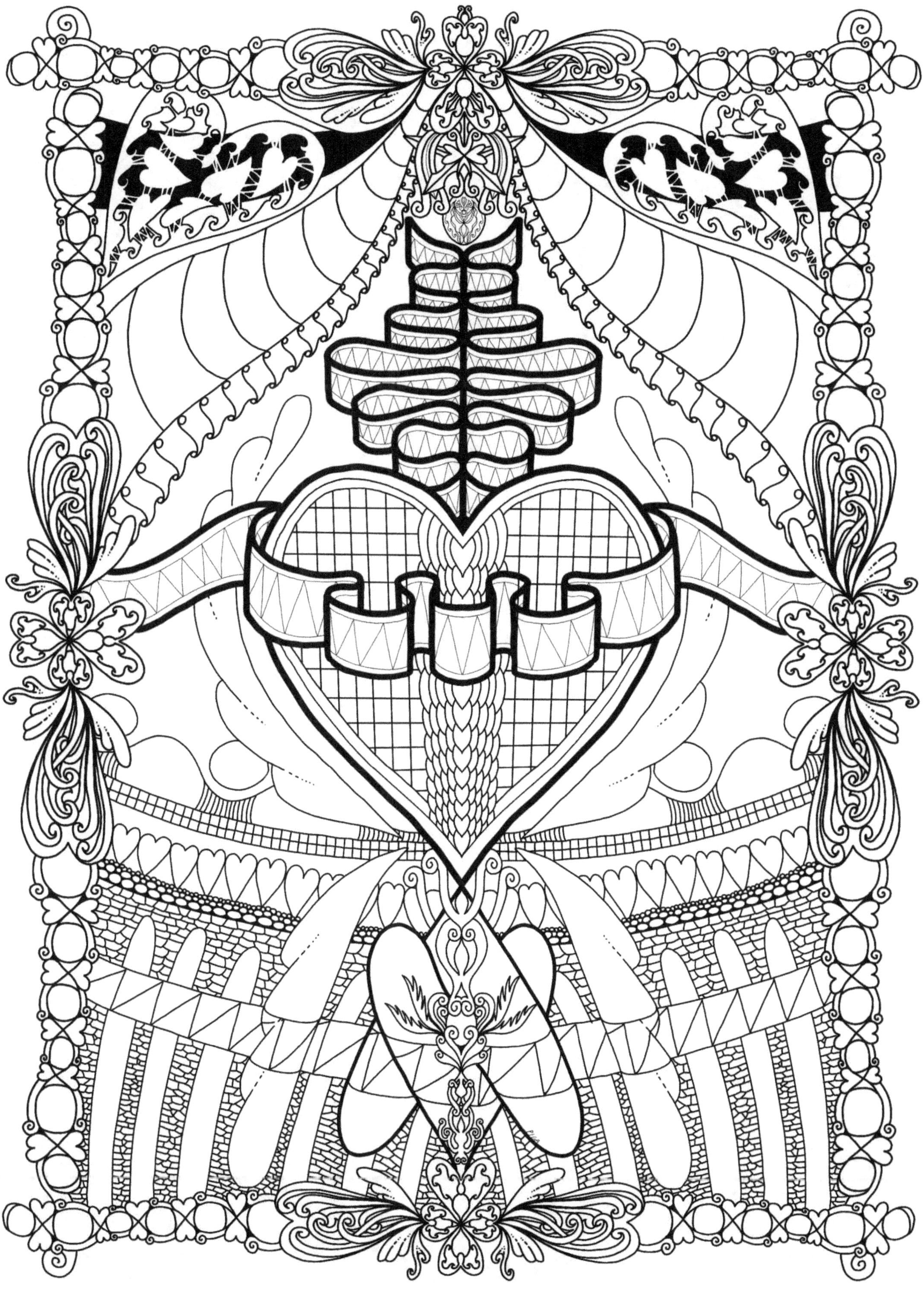

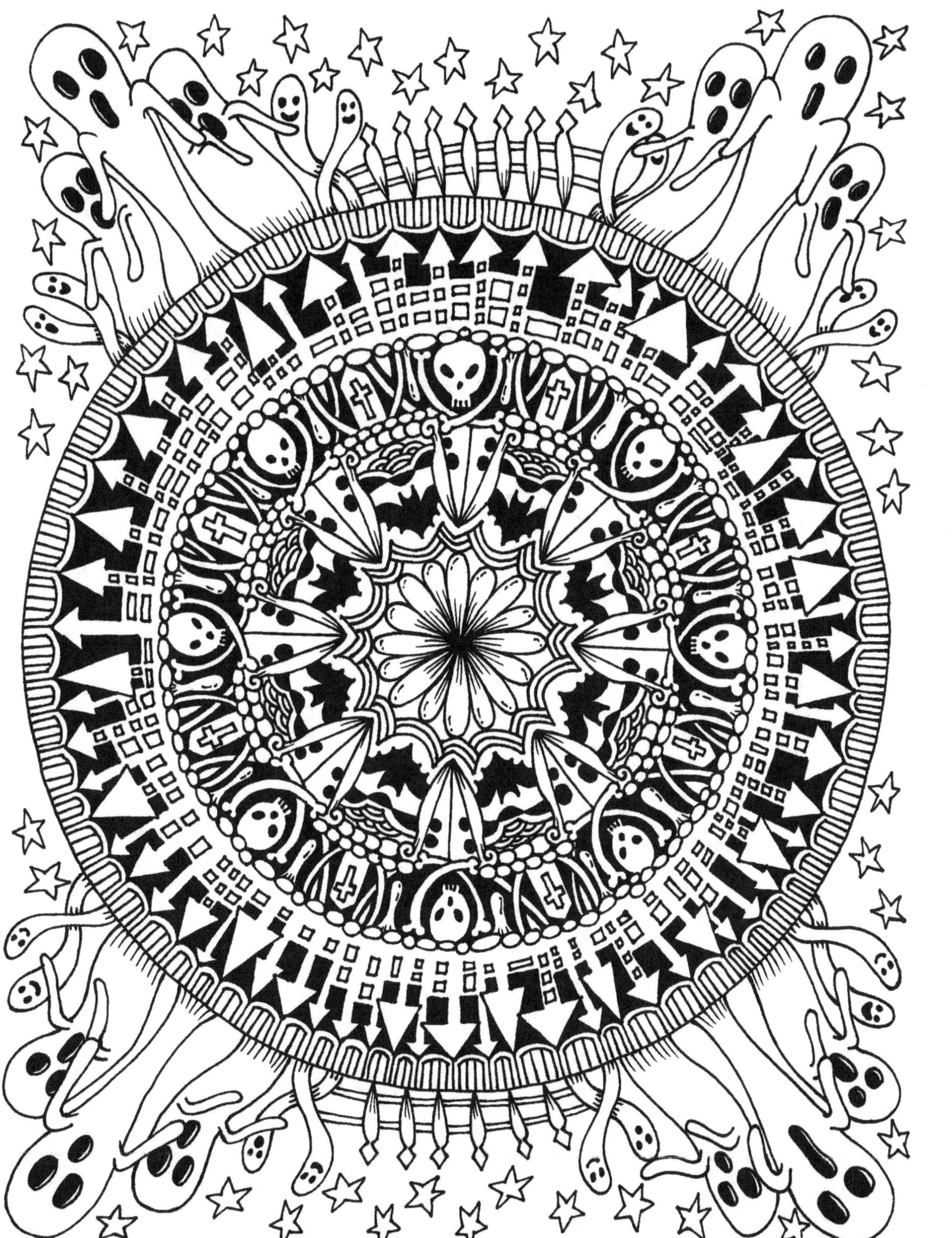

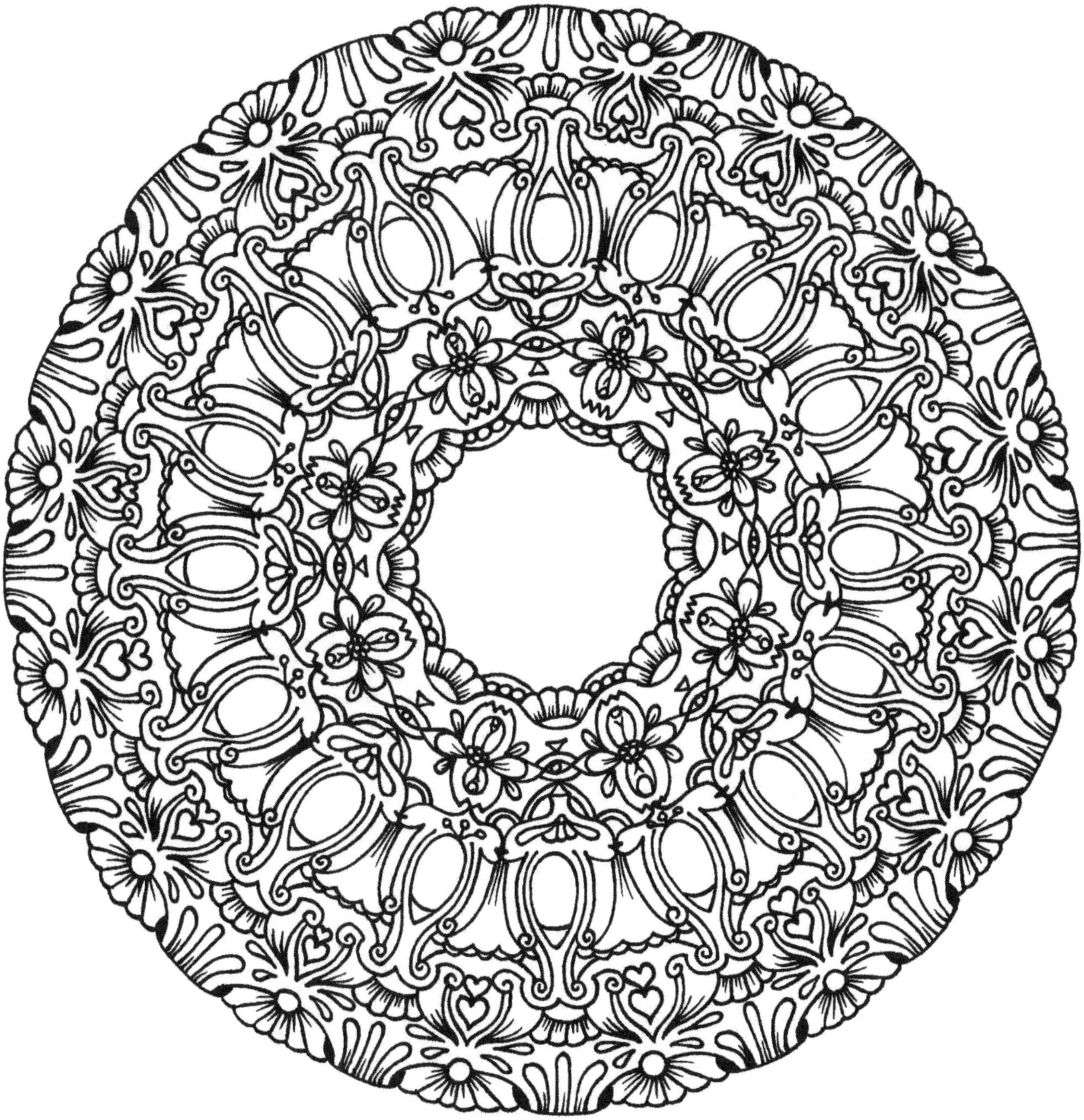

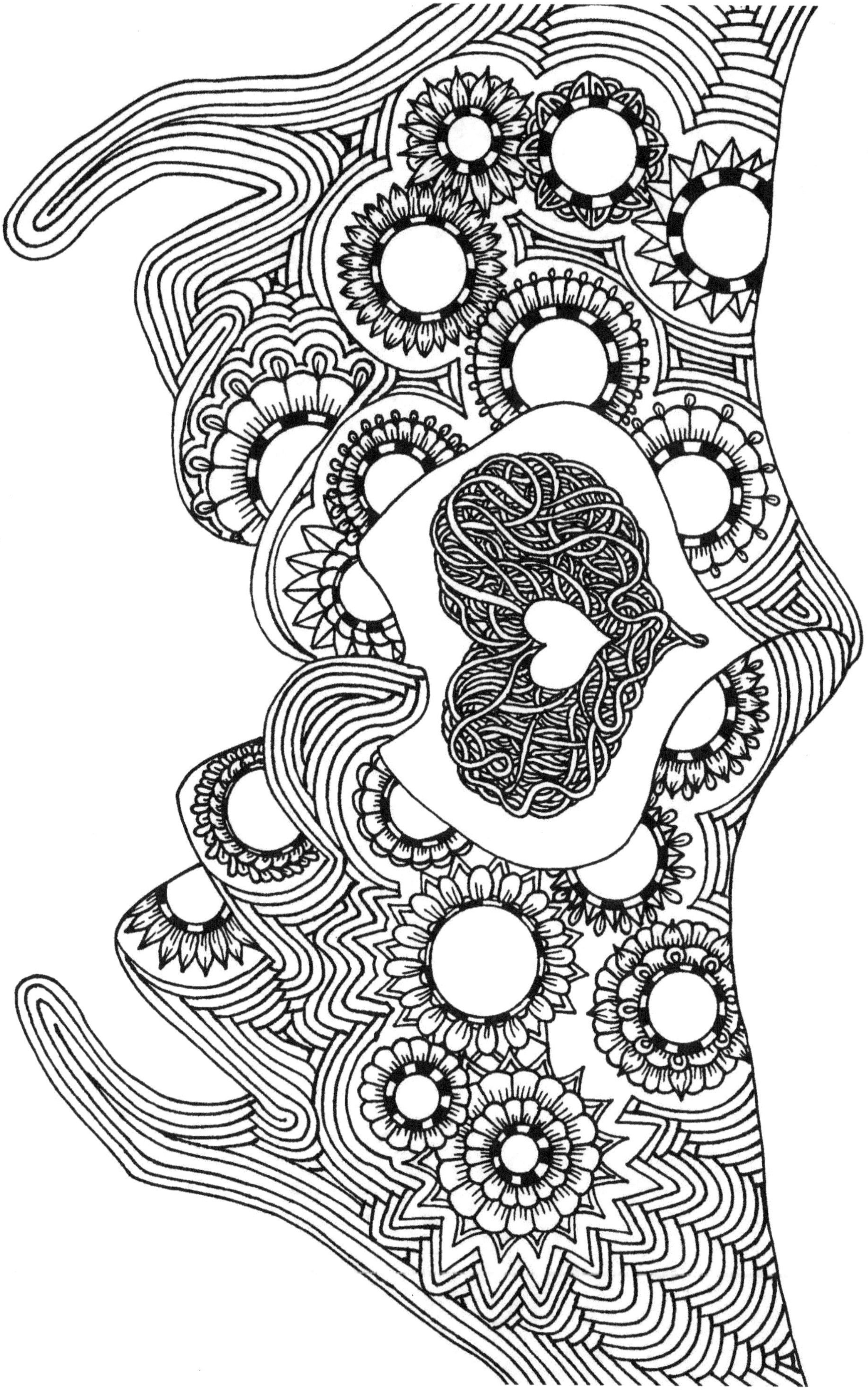

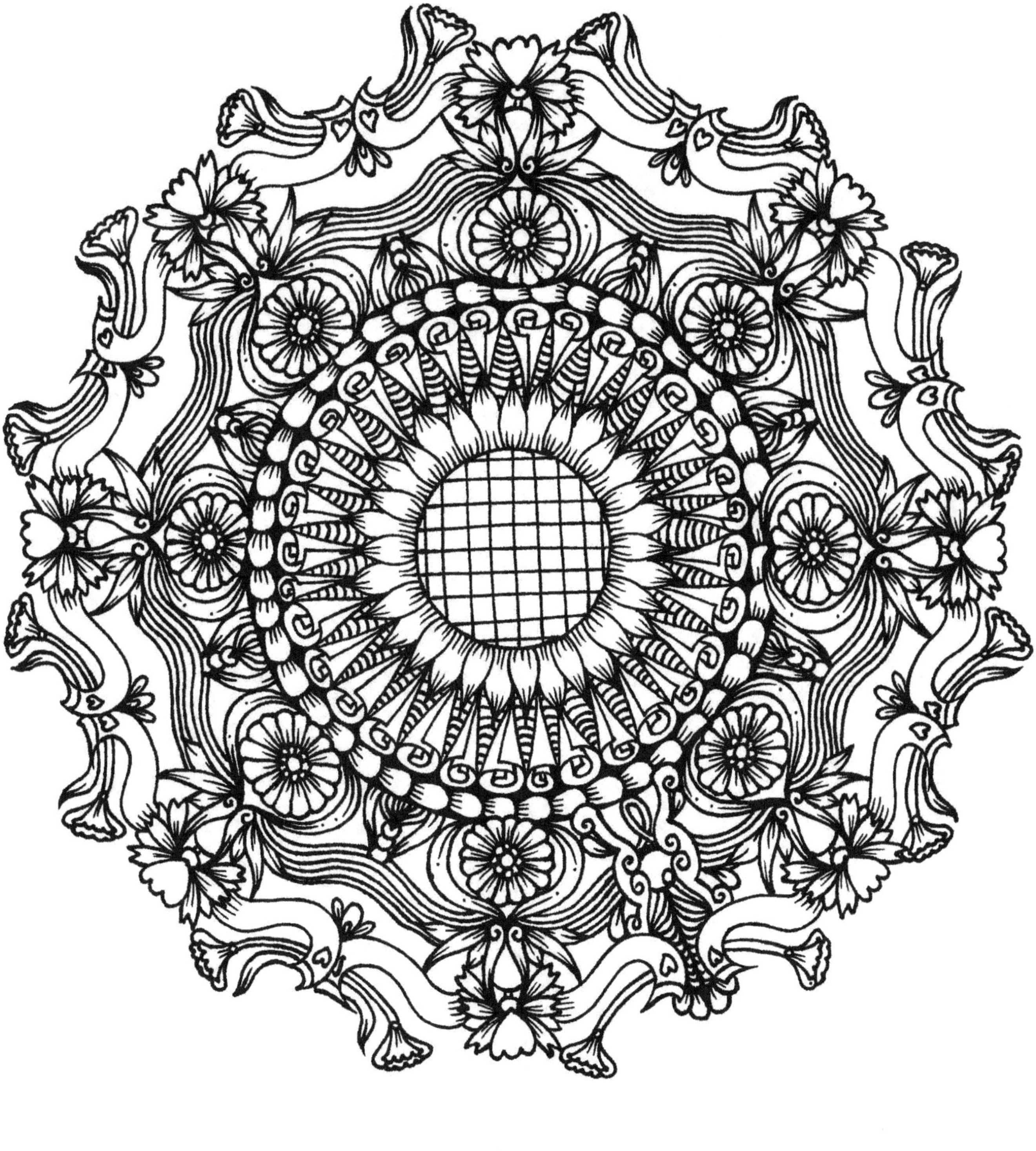

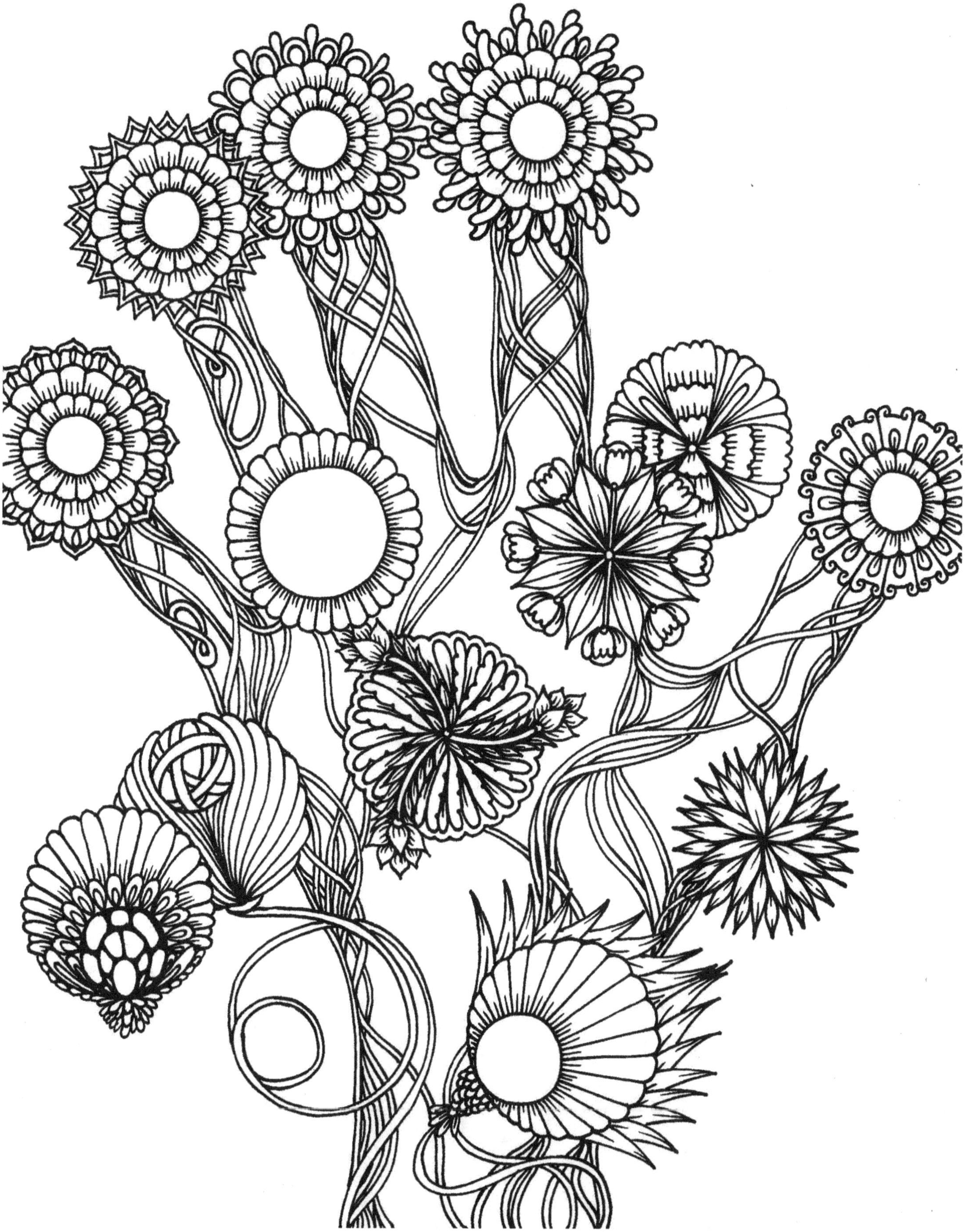

# THE PROTAGONISTS

BY PICA WU

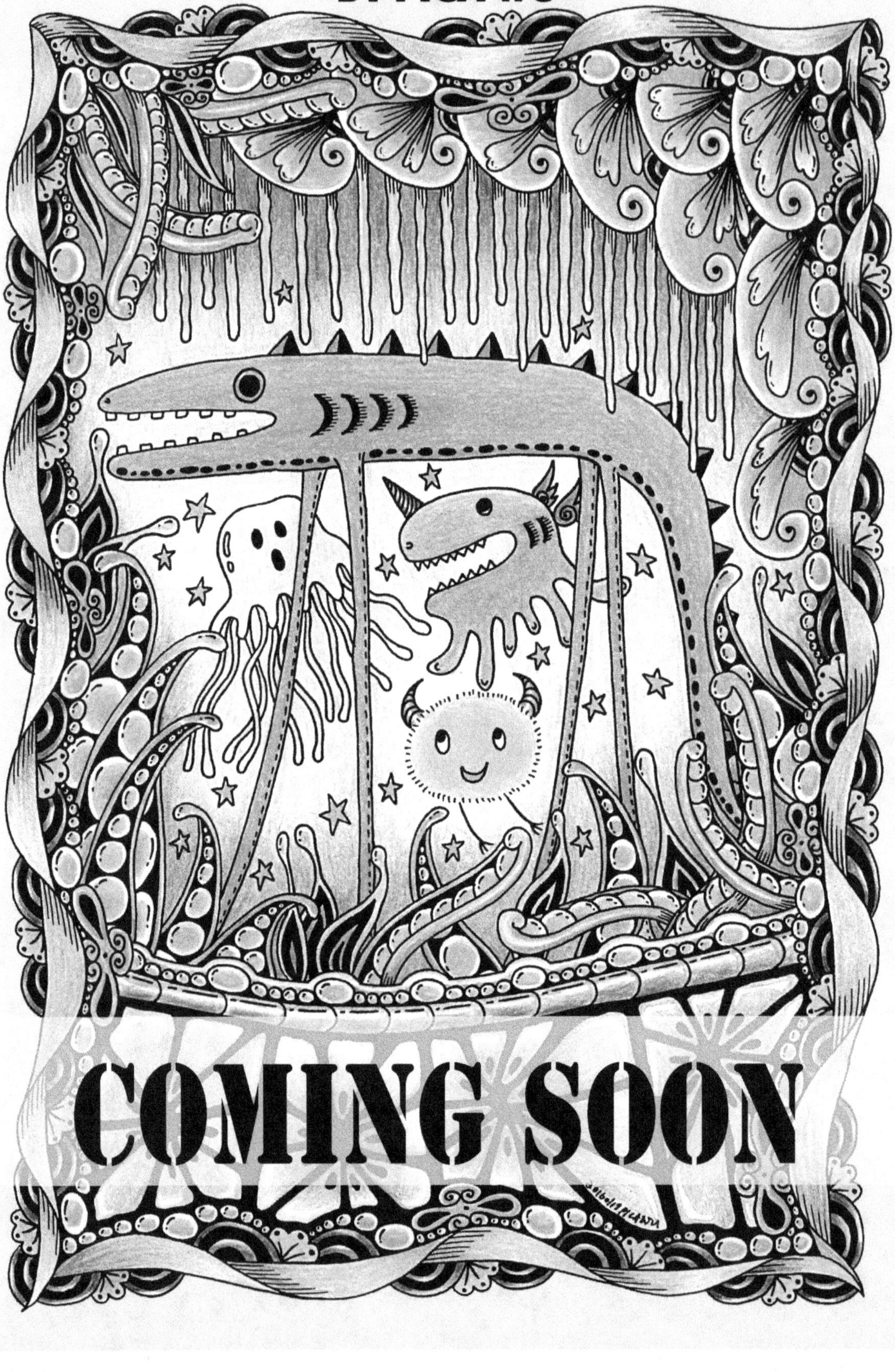

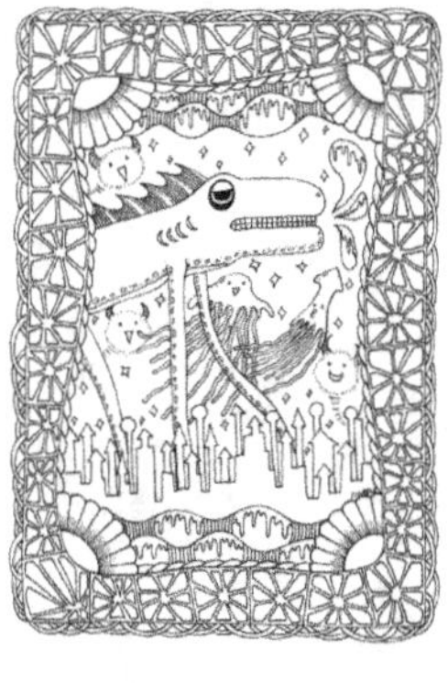
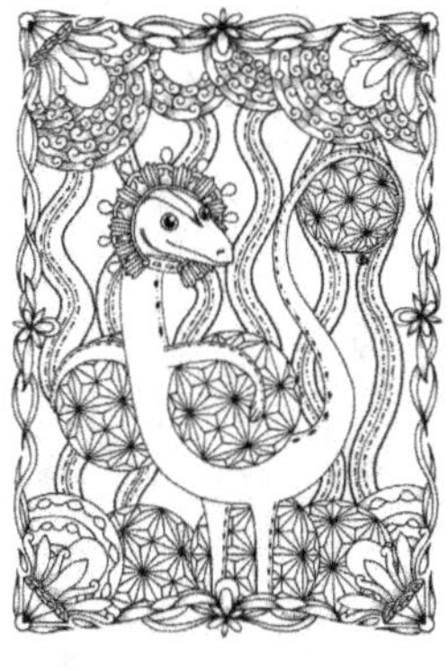
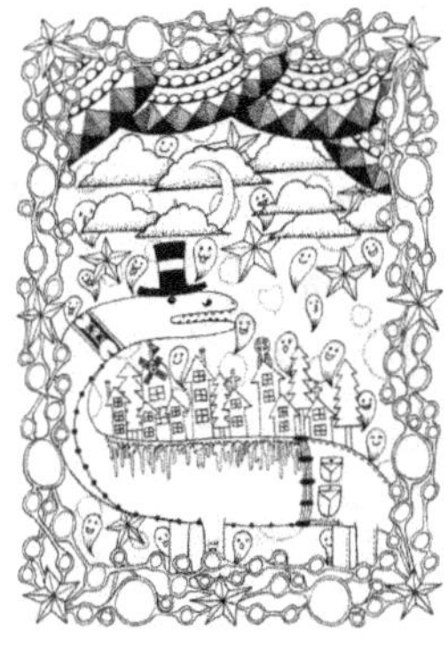
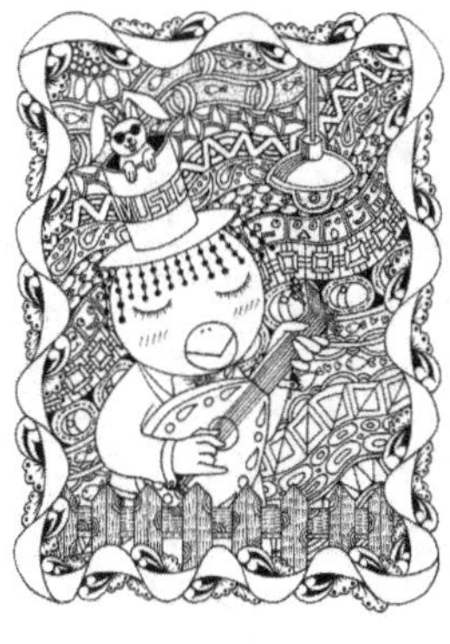
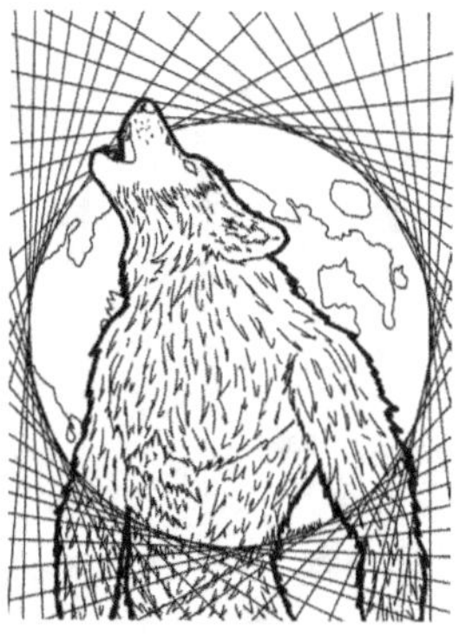
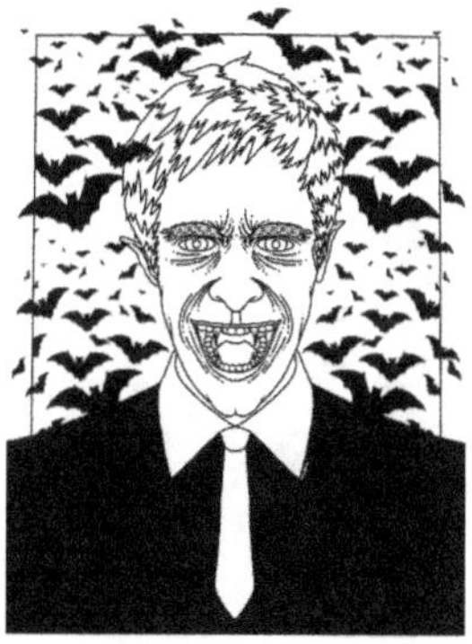
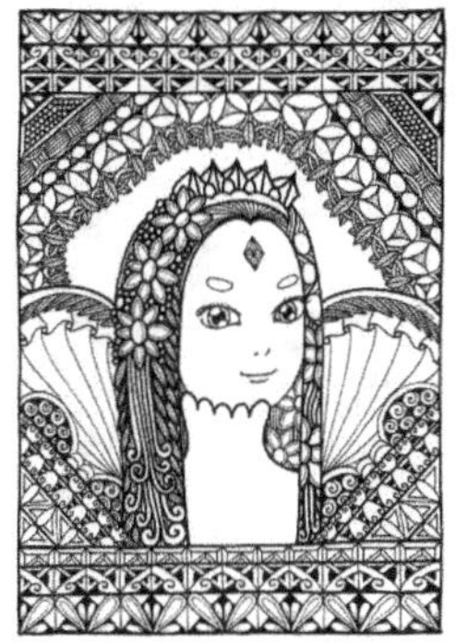
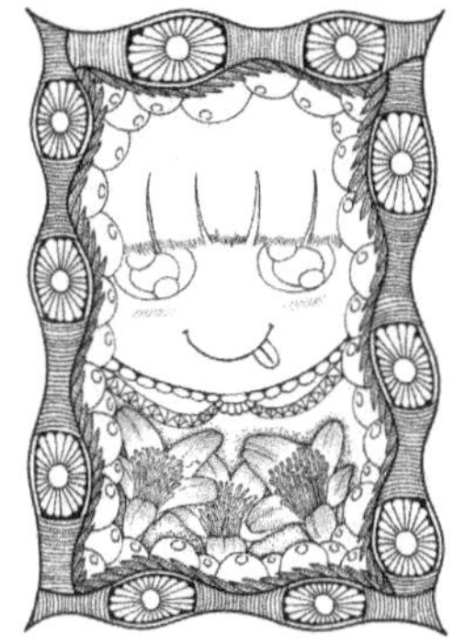
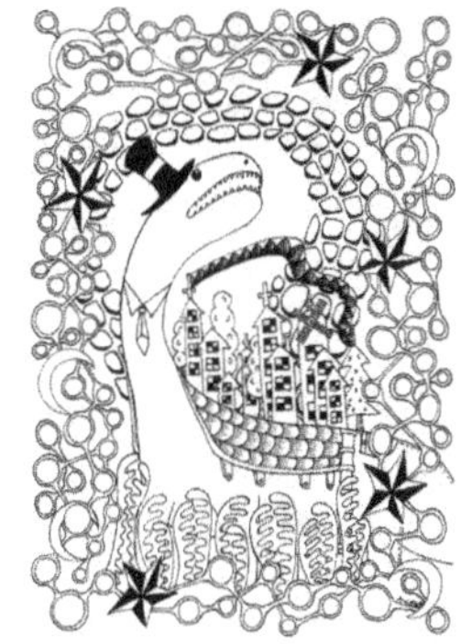
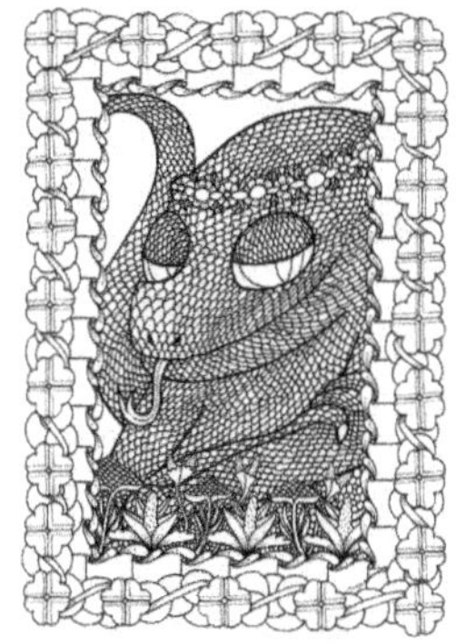
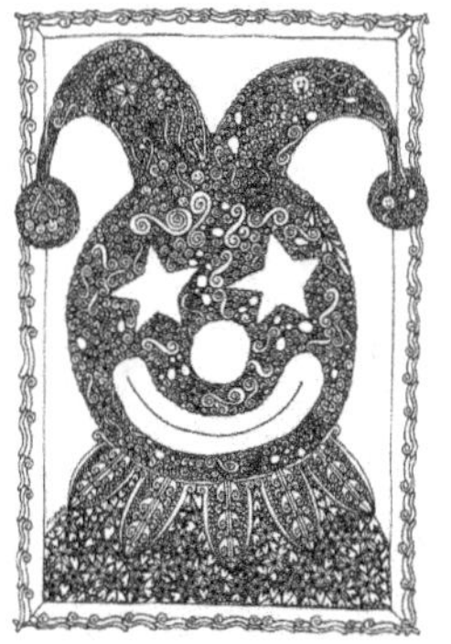
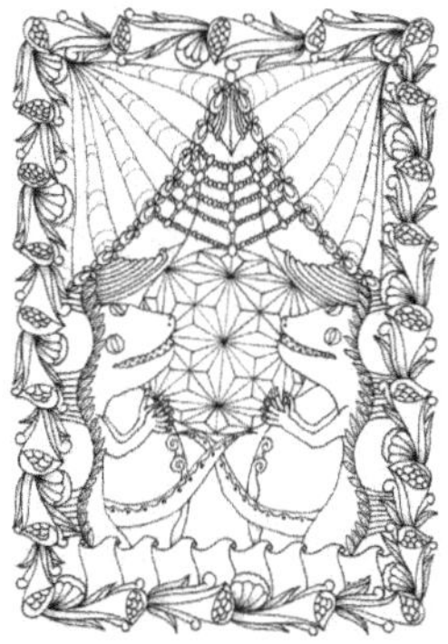
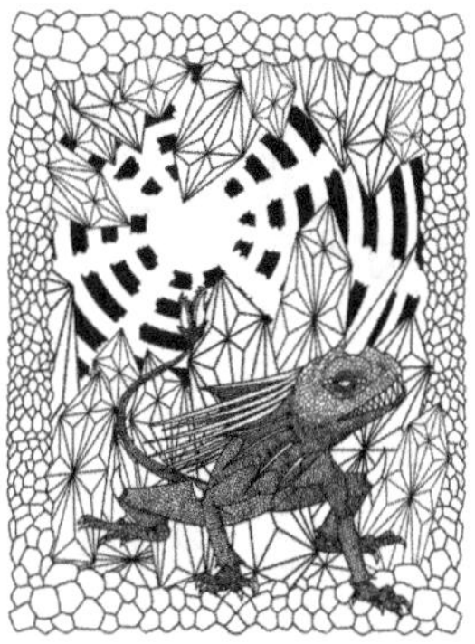
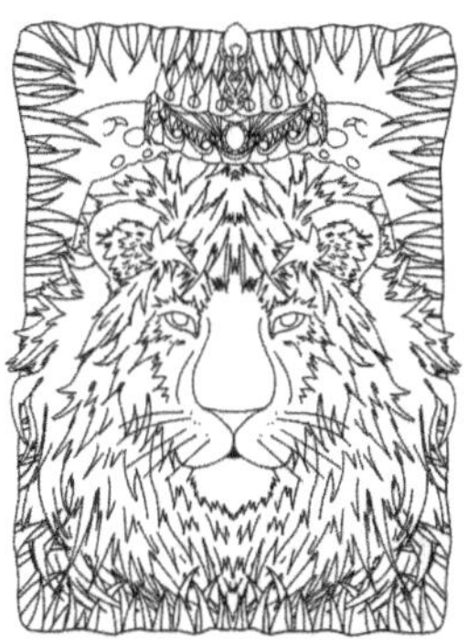
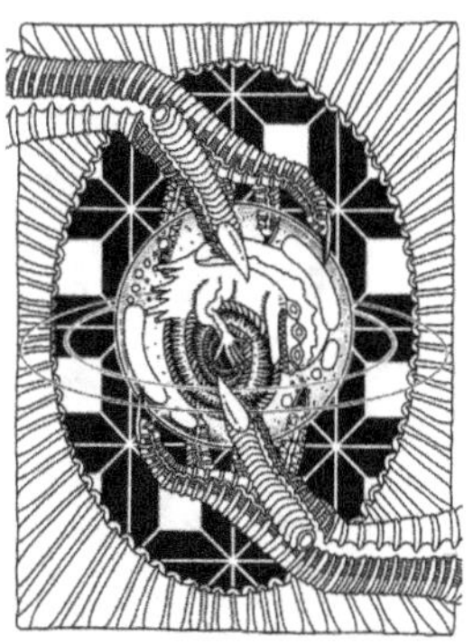
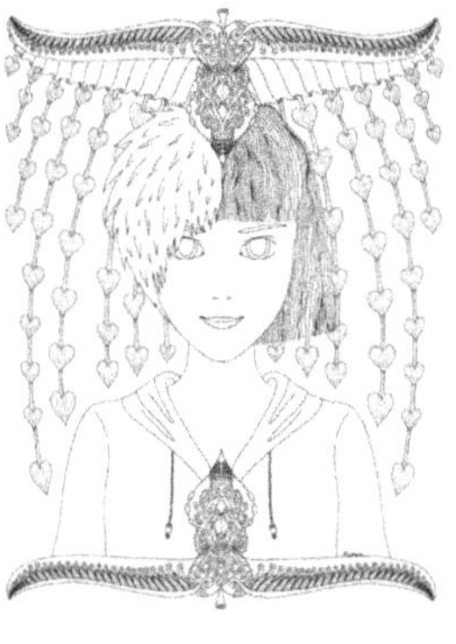
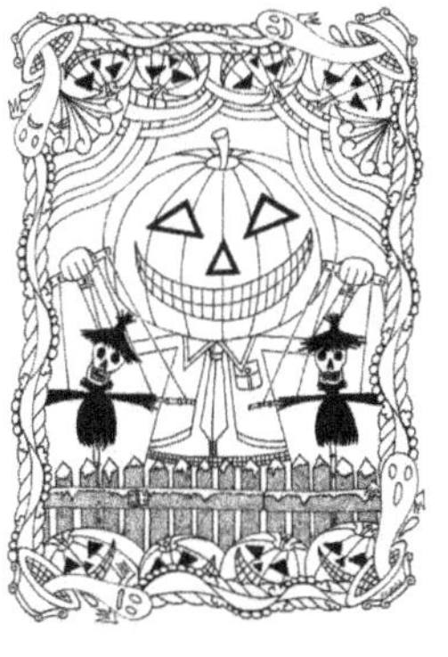
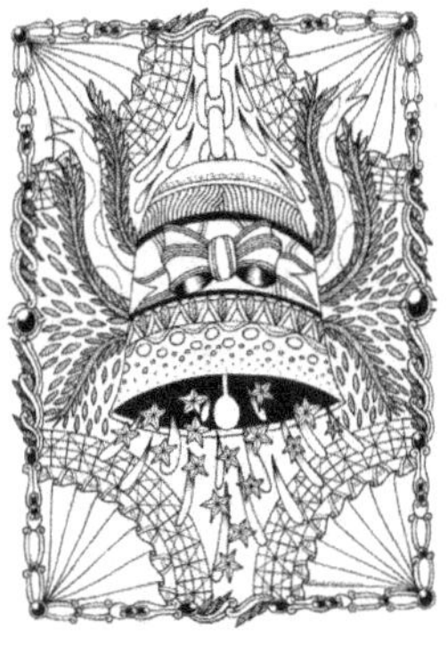
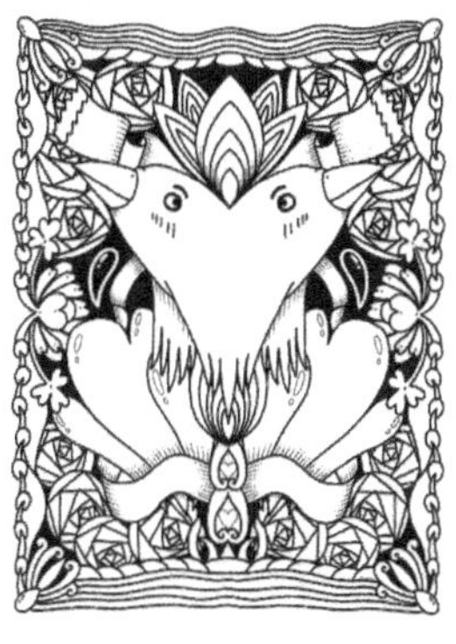
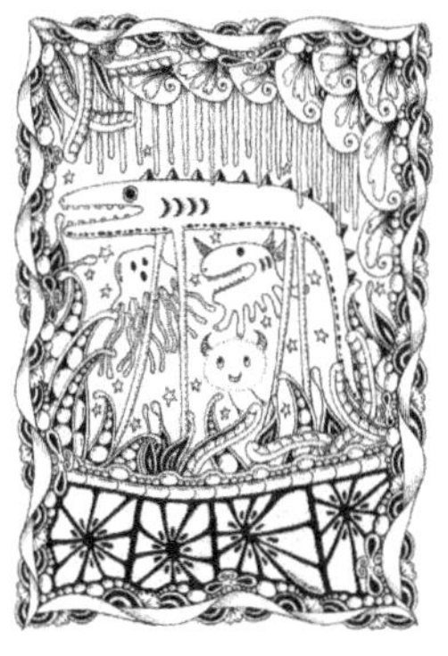
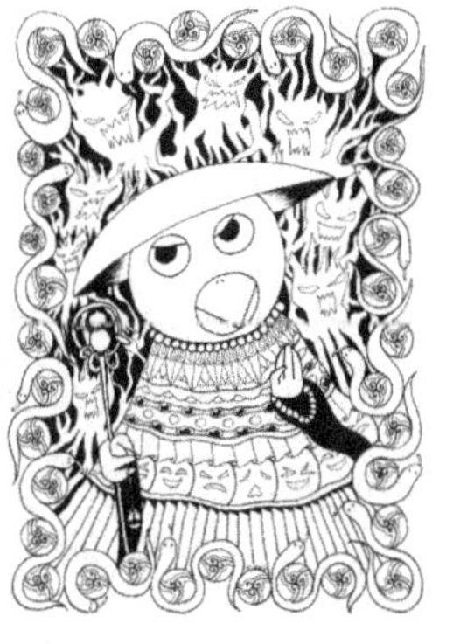
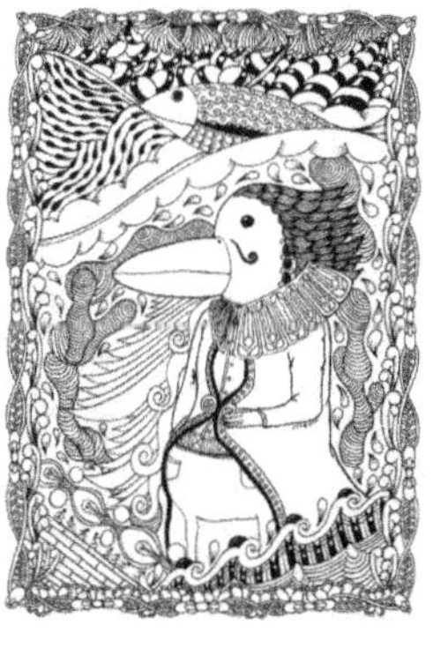
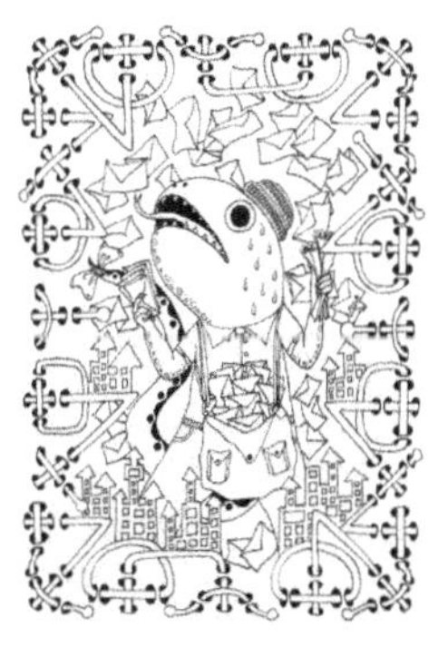
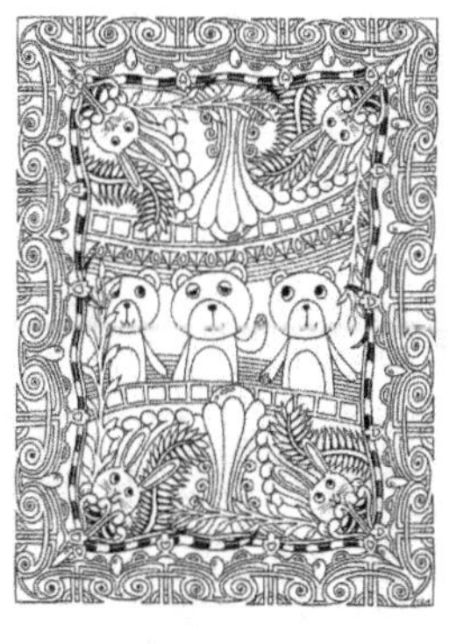
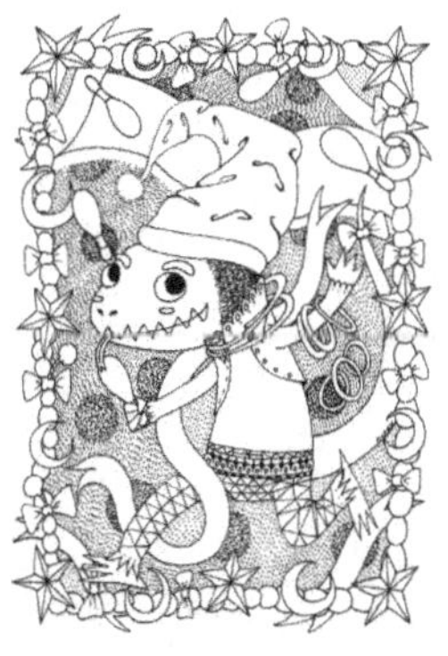

*Test your colors here on the samples from*
*"My Pocket Coloring Companion"*
*&*
*"My Coloring Companion"*

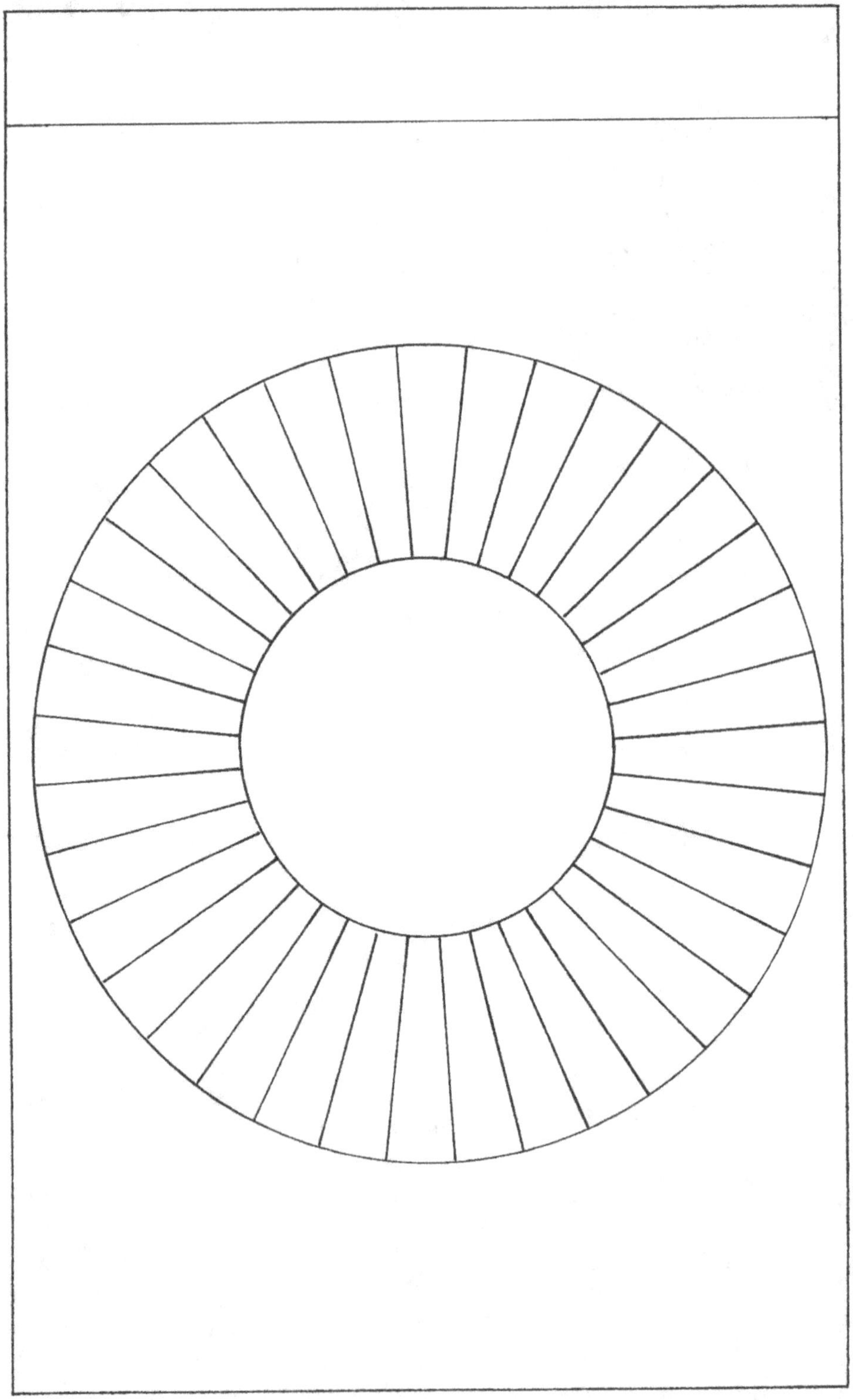

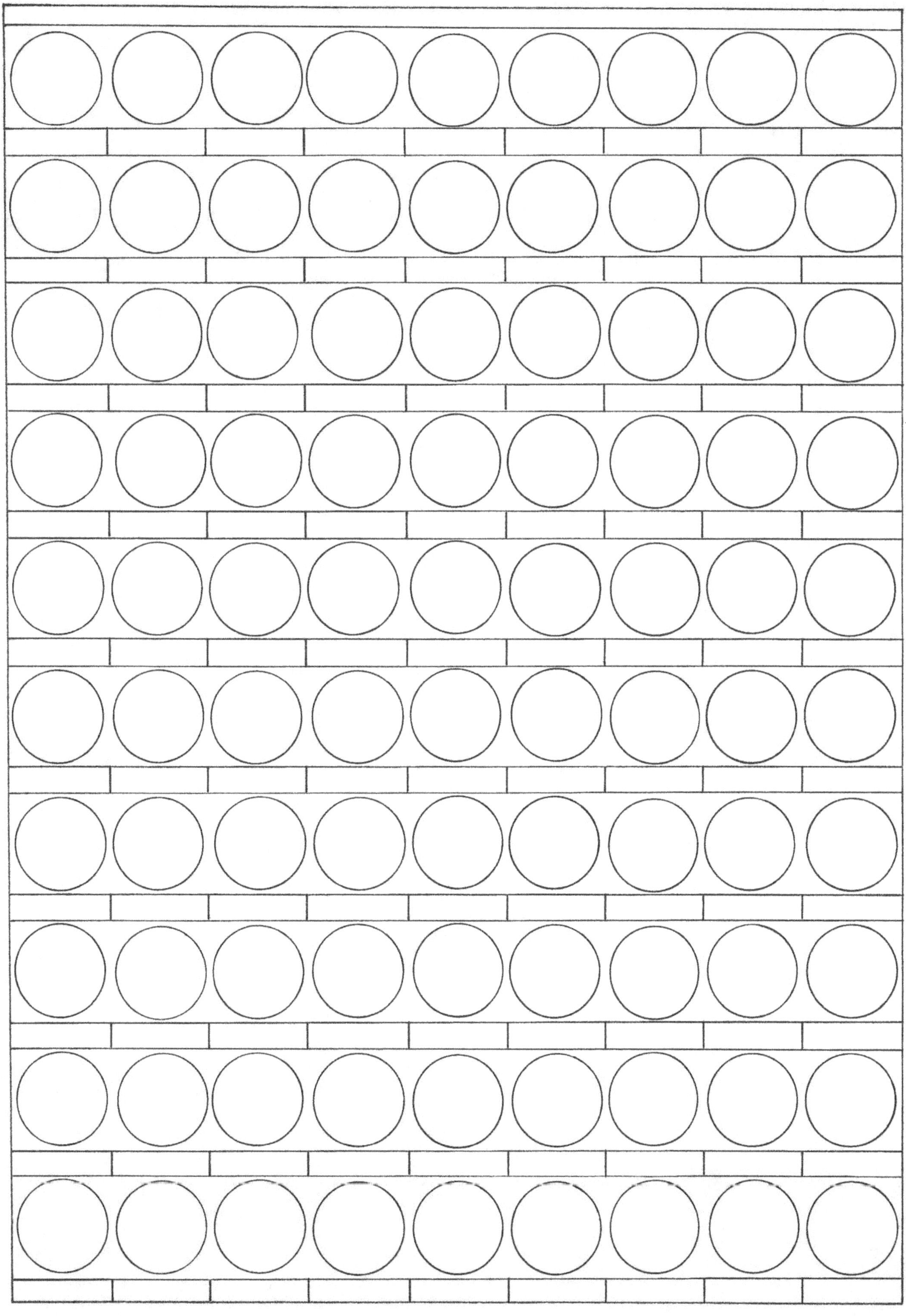

www.ingramcontent.com/pod-product-compliance
Lightning Source LLC
Chambersburg PA
CBHW080002230526
45470CB00008B/2828
* 9 7 8 8 7 9 3 3 8 5 8 8 7 *